Last Letter Home

Stories of War, Love and Remembrance

By
Josh Grossberg

Introduction by
Lt. Col. Tom Lasser, USA, (Ret.)

Last Letter Home

I have never advocated war except as a means of peace.
Ulysses S. Grant

Josh Grossberg

Preface

Those who fought in World War II – "The Greatest Generation," as they have become known – were brave beyond measure. But I've met too many men and women who served their country with honor to bestow that title to a single group of people. Maybe that's why, when I began to develop this collection of stories I've written over the years, mostly for the Daily Breeze newspaper in Southern California, my thoughts went not to a World War II veteran, but to a World War I vet, who was 105 years old when our paths crossed.

His name was Clifford Holliday and by the time we met in 2005, he was one of only a few remaining survivors of the War to End All Wars. He was too young to enlist when World War I broke out in 1917, so Holliday lied about his age, signed up as a bugle boy and spent his 17th birthday on the front line in France.

He avoided mustard gas poisoning by stuffing chemical-soaked rags into his mouth. He never knew what the chemical was, but he blamed it for a lifetime of health problems.

Even by the standards of war, World War I was horrific. And the experience soured Holliday to the concept of combat forever. His story is the first you'll read in this collection.

And that points to something about the people I write about in this book. Although each and every one of them was changed by the experiences they faced; they returned home with different attitudes about what they did and who they were.

Some spent years tortured by the experience, while others cherished their memories. Some re-enlisted, while others shunned the military until they reached middle age and felt the need to reconnect with others like themselves.

Not all of the people in this book faced combat. Some offered their support. Others sent their loved ones off to war. One became famous for celebrating the end of a war. But they all did their part to contribute to war efforts.

But different as they were, they all remained deeply patriotic and proud. Holliday died a couple of years later at 107. Many others are still with us. But each and every one of them sacrificed a part of themselves to help preserve our freedoms and way of life.

And we owe them a debt of gratitude.

I don't want to give any wrong impressions. I never served in the military. I was lucky enough to come of age after the draft ended and before the Selective Service program was reinstated. Vietnam was over and the Cold War was mostly being fought without guns.

But as I met people who served, I began to realize what they did for me and millions of others. I have no doubt that it is the wish of all the people in this book that future generations will be spared the things they had to endure. And if that time comes, it will be because of the sacrifices they made.

Many of the people you'll meet in this collection are no longer with us. But that only makes it more vital to tell and retell their stories. They were able to share many memories with me, and no matter how much time has passed, it's important to keep their stories alive.

And no matter if they served during World War II, Korea, Vietnam or the conflicts in the Middle East, they are all members of a great generation.

If you have a story to tell, I'd love to hear from you. Email me at info@lastletterhome.org

Or connect with others on Facebook at www.Facebook.com/LastLetterHome.

Josh Grossberg
Los Angeles

Foreword

I first met Josh Grossberg at a veterans event in 2003 in Redondo Beach, California. We chatted briefly and exchanged business cards and bumped into each other again over the years.

I've seen much of his work in the paper and other publications. As a retired soldier, Vietnam veteran, I was honored when he asked me to preview his new book, "Last Letter Home – Stories of War, Love and Remembrance".

This collection of living history is comprehensive and complete with honest testimony in a narrative, conversational style.

I am impressed with the honesty and sincere comments made by veterans of all ages and wars. Not really war stories but recollections and remembrances by ordinary Americans expressing themselves as they served in the armed forces to preserve our freedoms.

Josh paid special attention to let these veterans talk. Not only talk about themselves, their experiences, but talk about their buddies, their families and the little things that glue their stories together to make this a great book to read.

Most of these stories didn't involve social media or our current modern communications methods.

Much of these recollections came the old fashion way – buy virtue of letters. Putting pencil to paper. Hand written remembrances of life in the military and the oral history collected by Josh.

I especially liked the mix of veterans of all wars and all branches of the military. Some on the front lines, some in the sky and some in the rear with the gear. All expressing themselves, telling there stories. A collage of memories.

But many believing if there must be trouble, if there must be a fight, let it be in my day so my child may have peace in their day.

I heard once that the true soldier fights not because he hates what is in front of him but he fights because he loves those behind him.

Look for that in these stories.

I was a scared, young Army helicopter pilot in 1967. Eyes wide open but more often squeezed shut. I wish I had better observation skills, a better recollection of my experiences like many of these veterans.

My congratulations to all these great Americans for opening up to Josh and for telling us their stories. Hopefully we can all learn something about ourselves and our great country at the same time.

Remember, soldiers wear medals. Heroes wear the respect of a nation.

Lt. Col Tom Lasser, USA, ret

Redondo Beach, Calif

June 2012

Doughboy

(First published in 2005)

Before any of the twenty-somethings serving in today's military heard of Afghanistan – before their parents or even grandparents heard of Iraq – Clifford Holliday was fighting for his country.

Not in Vietnam or the Korean conflict. Not in World War II. The Southern California resident was slogging through European trenches during World War I.

Holliday is 104, older than airplanes, penicillin and talking pictures.

"Practically everything we use in the modern world has been developed since I was born," he said.

His wife died nearly 30 years ago. His only child has

died of old age. His 15 brothers and sisters are also gone. But Holliday is still alert, still has a few original teeth and is still able to amble around the small home he's lived in since 1948.

He spends his days reading newspapers and writing. He rarely watches television (first broadcast when Holliday was nearly 30).

Even after all these years, he has little taste for images of war.

"I had all the war I want," he said. "I don't want to see, hear or smell any more war."

Stagecoaches were still running when Holliday was born in September 1898 in rural Canada.

"I was a bread-and-butter boy on a farm," he said.

When Archduke Ferdinand was assassinated in 1914 signaling the beginning of what was then known as the Great War, Holliday wanted to join the fight. But at 16, he was too young to join the Canadian Army, so he lied about his age and enlisted in the service as a bugle boy, a position that exists now only in the movies.

"They seemed to have forgot about that classification," he said.

He celebrated his 17th birthday on the front lines in France, but left the Army when he was 19 after being hit in the face with shrapnel.

Of the 600,000 Canadians who served during the war, Holliday is one of only a dozen still living (2 million Americans also served). It was a difficult war, with troops dug into trenches for months at a time. And German troops employed mustard gas, a particularly nasty chemical that caused a slow and painful death. For protection, Holliday was given a rag treated with an unknown chemical.

"I don't think we can appreciate how that war was fought," said Janice Summerby, a spokeswoman with Veterans Affairs Canada. "Some of them served for four years in trenches. And the ones who survived are classic gentlemen. They haven't let what they lived through overwhelm their lives."

In some ways, it was what happened in that war that led to the current situation in the Middle East, said John Novicki, president of the Great War Association.

"One of the reasons we're in Iraq right now is because of the poison gas that could be released by a nut," he said. "Back then, it wasn't a question of if. They were already doing it. They were really exposed to all that stuff."

Holliday managed to get through the war without exposure to gas, but he does have scarred lungs, which he blames on whatever those supposedly protective rags were soaked with.

His experience left him wary of war. He said he would reserve judgment on the Iraq war until the dust settles.

"It's a little too early to know," he said. "This thing could escalate into a world guerrilla war against the U.S. and its allies. If it has any."

Leaving Canada on the advice of a friend who promised good jobs in the Golden State, Holliday headed south after the war. The trip took him six days. His work as an electrician led him to install the first sound system at Columbia Studios. He also wired movie theaters for speakers. It was a job that put him in close proximity to some of the day's biggest stars.

"I've seen Douglas Fairbanks and Mary Pickford," he said. "Ingrid Bergman sat next to me in the cafeteria. Will Rogers and I shook hands. He was a great guy."

That Will Rogers died in 1935 doesn't mean Holliday can't remember the great humorist clearly. Holliday can close his eyes and recall some of the smallest details – names, dates, snippets of conversation.

His first car was a 1916 Cleveland.

One of his early jobs paid $1.70 an hour, which he considered rather generous.

He got married in 1920.

His house cost $10,500.

The first movie he saw starred Charlie Chaplin, but he doesn't remember the title.

"When I went to the movies, it was black and white without any voice. When the sound came out, that was a whole different world," he said.

The walls of Holliday's home are covered with plaques and proclamations from civic organizations and community leaders. One of them, now fading with age, congratulates him for turning 90.

If there's one annoying part about being 104, it's everybody asking what his secret for long life is. He's got a couple of answers.

"Wild women."

"Plenty of hard work."

"I don't feel pain and I don't panic. I've been in perfect health all my life."

And then, rather cryptically he adds, "The secret of life is everything is an electrical phenomenon."

The road ahead may be shorter than the one behind him, but Holliday doesn't have any plans to stop reading the paper every day or clipping out articles and highlighting the interesting parts. He stays away from television, but still manages to keep up on current events. And he knows that some young man or woman fighting today will grow old as he did. And he knows that whatever the world dishes out, people will learn to handle it.

"One thing you got to remember is your nature prepares you for the time you live in," he said. "Twenty-five or 100, you still adapt for the time."

The Atomic Veterans

(First published in 2006)

It sounded like a shotgun blast. To Rod Rohrberg, it looked like the end of the world.

Rohrberg was standing on the deck of a ship just 6 miles away when the world's fifth atomic bomb detonated in 1946. Rohrberg can still feel the wave of the blast as it rocked his Navy ship like a bath toy.

"It was scary," he said. "It was awesome being there."

World War II was over, but the government needed to better understand the vast power unleashed by nuclear weapons. Operation Crossroad near the Bikini Islands was the first series of tests conducted after similar bombs fell on Japan at the end of the war. The second bomb in the test – and the first ever to be detonated underwater – was code named Baker. Science understood little about radiation and Rohrberg was only 20 at the time and knew even less. The men on his ship wore no protection from the blast.

"We just turned away until we heard the boom," Rohrberg said. "Then we looked at it. We saw a steam cloud coming. We thought it was a tidal wave."

A few hours later, the ship moved closer to the blast site until it reached ground zero. Rohrberg didn't know it at the time, but his body was being bombarded with radiation.

"We had that on our bodies," he said. "We didn't know how bad it would be. Nobody did."

A Geiger counter confirmed he was radioactive. The remedy was to keep scrubbing until it went away.

"We took showers until we were click ... click ... click," he said, spacing the clicks about a half-second apart.

Rohrberg stayed in the Navy until 1954. With a degree in civil engineering, he opened a company that helped design the Apollo moon mission, the space shuttle, the Strategic Defense Initiative and many other space programs.

But what happened that day would come back to haunt him. He had muscle spasms and became forgetful. And then he was diagnosed with cancer – the first of three times he would come down with the disease.

"I've been sick since 1965," he said. "For five or six years, no one knew why."

And then a doctor told him something disturbing. Of all the men who were there that day in 1946, most were dead.

"He said I was one of only three alive," Rohrberg said.

"There were 44 of us."

He endured years of chemotherapy and operations. Several of his organs had to be removed.

"All I have inside me is the bare essentials," he said.

Atomic tests lasted until 1992. In all, 750,000 men were involved.

"We were there to follow orders and we followed orders," said R.J. Ritter, commander of the National Association of Atomic Veterans. "They needed to know the atomic radiation effects on equipment and personnel. They needed to know if somebody close could carry on his duties and still fight."

During the Cold War, when tensions with the USSR – another nuclear power – ran high, such tests were important, Ritter said.

"We were all guinea pigs," he said. "We were all test subjects. In those days, it was in the interest of national security. We have atomic veterans dying every day as a result."

Rohrberg built a successful career and raised a loving family. But he wonders what he might have accomplished if he hadn't been sidelined by illness so many times.

"Where could we be if I hadn't been sick for 20 of the last 40 years?" he said. "But I work seven days a week. It doesn't do any good to cry."

And while he hasn't enjoyed being ill, Rohrberg said it was an honor to serve his country.

"I'm a God-bless-America guy," he said. "I would do it

again. How many guys stood at a Geiger counter when it (went off) and lived to tell about it?"

Surrender

(First published in 2005)

Reliable news was slow to reach the USS Nicholas. Stationed out in the Pacific, its crew didn't hear about the atomic bombs dropped on Japan until Aug. 15, 1945, more than a week after the first one.

And on the same day, when the radio crackled that Japan had surrendered, the crew first heard it not from Allied forces, but from the Japanese themselves.

It was the end of the war, but for Ed Sokolski, 83, and the crew of the Nicholas, the adventure was far from over. Even after fighting the Japanese in intense battles, the California resident and his shipmates were given the task of picking up Japanese dignitaries and ferrying them to the USS Missouri, where the peace treaty was signed Sept. 2.

25

"(Adm. William) Halsey chose us," he said. "We went into harbor in Tokyo with a Japanese destroyer. We didn't know what the heck they would do. Fortunately, they really decided to surrender."

It wasn't easy playing host to the former enemy, but it was something the crew did with professionalism, he said.

"We were courteous to them," he said.

Sokolski kept a book filled with black-and-white photos of his ship and the men he served with, but there aren't any of Sokolski because he was the one holding the camera.

The Missouri was taller than the Nicholas, so Sokolski didn't have a good vantage point for the historic event, but he took pictures of many of the key players: Halsey, Adm. Chester Nimitz and Japanese Foreign Minister Mamoru Shigemitsu.

"China, Russia, there were representatives of every country in creation," Sokolski said.

Although the crew of the Nicholas was apprehensive about having Japanese dignitaries on the ship, Sokolski said that after they surrendered, there were no problems.

"Once the war was over, they gave us no trouble," he said. "I went into a store (in Tokyo) and (the shopkeeper) started giving me things. He was surprised when I gave him money."

Japan was not known for treating prisoners well. And when Sokolski's ship picked up some captive Japanese soldiers before the war ended, the prisoners were nervous.

"When we picked them up, they thought we would shoot

them. But the guys gave them cigarettes and something to eat. They couldn't believe it."

Although he had been involved in several conflicts before the war ended, Sokolski said life on a ship was better than fighting on land.

"On ship, it was clean," he said. "If you were lucky and didn't get hit, it was an easy operation."

But life on a ship during the war wasn't always easy. For some me danger remained even after the enemy surrendered.

"After the war was over, guys were still getting shot and killed," said Louis A. Gomez a California resident who joined the USS Terror after a kamikaze attack on the vessel had killed 43 men.

And while parties raged stateside, it was business as usual for men at sea.

"I never had a celebration," said 83-year-old Ed Price. "What should I do, stand on my head? At least I knew I wasn't going to be in another invasion."

Sokolski was happy the war ended when it did. If Japan hadn't surrendered after the atomic bombs were dropped, the Allies would have invaded the island nation. The results, he said, would have been catastrophic for American men.

"When they surrendered, what a relief," he said. "They fight until death. We would have lost 300,000 men. That was a tough decision Truman had to make."

Sokolski spent several more months at sea until finally docking at Terminal Island in Los Angeles. "They threw us a party. There were dancers and sorority girls."

His time in the Navy wasn't up, so Sokolski spent several more months in the service, but he managed to get stationed near his family in New York. Until his discharge, he drove military dignitaries around.

"And that's how the whole thing ended," he said.

Ghost of War

(First published in 2003)

Dick Peterson had already been on 23 successful runs against the Nazis in his B-24 bomber. One more and the 20-year-old would have been able to return home from the battle for Europe during World War II.

But his plane was hit by enemy fire and Peterson had to parachute into a field in occupied France.

"They decided to turn me over to the Germans," he said of the people who found him badly injured. "They couldn't give me the medical attention I needed."

Peterson finally made it home, but not before enduring almost two years as a prisoner of war, where he was subjected to harsh treatment, forced marches in the dead of winter and near starvation.

Peterson was among the thousands of men who were captured by the enemy during wartime. He and others like him are honored each year on National POW/MIA Day.

It's a time for the nation to remember those who, like Peterson, were captured by the enemies of the United States in conflicts around the globe, along with thousands more whose fate remains unknown.

William McMahon of Manhattan Beach, Calif., also was captured during a flying mission in World War II. The date was Jan. 28, 1944, and McMahon had just turned 19. He was shot down over Anzio and picked up by Italian fascists, who didn't have any intention of taking him prisoner.

"I understood enough Italian to know they were going to kill us," he said.

It was the Germans who first became his saviors and then his tormentors. The Italians handed McMahon to the Nazis, who put him in a series of camps where he too nearly starved to death.

They didn't know each other at the time, but Peterson and McMahon would wind up working together at Hughes Aircraft and both became members of American Ex-Prisoners of War.

During the early days of his capture, Peterson was shuttled around Germany in cramped boxcars and even spent four days crowded into the hold of an ocean freighter, where the men had to take turns sitting down. McMahon was on the ship too.

"They would let 10 or 15 guys on deck to relieve

themselves," he said. "Two guys jumped overboard, but I don't know why. They were shot by the Germans and we were miles from shore."

Later, he was handcuffed to another man and forced to run to a prison camp miles away. Injured men would slow healthy men down and both would be killed. Peterson still has a scar from the bayonet that a German thrust into his arm.

"The captain kept yelling, 'show no mercy,' " he recalled. "If you were a guy with a bum leg, you fell behind."

The camp was known as Stalag Luft Four, where many fliers were locked up.

"They called it a punishment camp," McMahon said. "Things were not good there."

Both men stayed there for a while until the Germans once again made them move. For Peterson, that meant a three-month march through the woods in mid-winter.

"We had dysentery," he said. "Everybody got sick. We lost a number of people who couldn't keep up."

But when the end of the war was nearing, the young German guards were replaced by older men resigned to defeat. Deciding they'd be better off with Americans than Russians, they surrendered on May 1, 1945.

Now, more than 60 years later, the ghosts of the war still haunt both men. They suffered from nightmares for years and even now have health problems linked to the harsh treatment they received.

"I have arthritic problems associated with malnutrition," Peterson said. "I have a heart condition that can be traced back to that."

"A lot of these guys wind up with some illness," McMahon said.

The holiday, which occurs on the third Friday in September, was founded in 1979 and honors not just those who served and were captured or never came home, but also their families.

"We hope everyone pauses for just a moment to be reminded that there are still people out there who have suffered greatly because this nation asked them to step forward," said Larry Greer, a spokesman for the Pentagon's POW/MIA Office. "Some of them never returned, some returned proudly, some broken. And all have families who have endured just as much pain. We hope everyone will recognize that."

World War II saw the most men captured or lost – 78,000 men and women who fought in that conflict are still not accounted for. Each war since then has also had soldiers face similar fates, but the numbers continue to shrink. Even during the Cold War, which many consider a bloodless battle, 126 men never came home, according to Pentagon statistics.

The government remains committed to finding out what happened to any serviceman or woman who is still missing, employing more than 600 people whose job it is to locate them.

"We have a budget of about $103 million a year to carry out this mission," Greer said. "Some people say it's not enough, some say too much. But this country has decided this is what we need to do to carry out the commitment to the servicemen and their families."

It wasn't until the last few years that Peterson or McMahon talked to their families about what happened. But now they participate in discussions and speak to groups about their captures.

Both said they'd be willing to once again don uniforms if their country needed them.

"If Uncle Sam wants you to do something, you do it," McMahon said. "But I don't think I'd get into an airplane."

For Peterson, memories drift to the acts of humanity – the sharing of food, even the young Nazi who helped remove something that had wrapped around his neck. The one thing that still nags at him is the guilt he felt when he stole a loaf of bread.

"This bothers me to this day," Peterson said. "This German had a sack and I knew there was bread in it. So I took a razor blade and cut through it and took the bread. That poor bastard went hungry so I could eat."

Armed Forces Day

(First published in 2006)

Each time their country needed them, the men and women of the armed forces answered the call. From Lexington and Concord to Fallujah and Baghdad, they served bravely and with honor. Each veteran has a unique story to tell, but as generations pass, many remain unheard.

To commemorate Armed Forces Day – which is rarely celebrated anymore, but comes the week before Memorial Day – veterans from World War II, Korea, Vietnam, Desert Storm, and the recent Iraq war, sat down to recall their days of service. They all risked their lives, but they know they were the lucky ones. They came home. These are their stories in their own words.

Josh Grossberg

Robert Metcalf – World War II

After he was drafted to serve in Gen. George Patton's 3rd Army, Robert Metcalf lived through the Battle of the Bulge and witnessed some of man's cruelest acts. But with a combination of luck and good fortune, Metcalf made it through.

First classified 4F, his status was upgraded every time he was needed to perform a different task. He smiled wryly about how even getting shot might have been something of a lucky break.

I started by guarding Japanese kids I went to high school with. I still remember one of my classmates asking me over the fence, "Are you going to shoot me with that thing?"

Off to guard Italian POWs – about as dangerous as a St. Bernard pup. Then to Wisconsin because I had somehow become 1A. From there to the infantry. Lots of training and then the Bulge happened. The next thing I know I was on a quiet sector of the front. I don't know why they called it quiet; they threw everything at us except Volkswagens.

Combat was a blur to me. I fought and walked from Belgium to Czechoslovakia. Some time, in the midst of it, I got a million-dollar wound. It was a machine gun bullet through my right leg. It sent me to a series of hospitals. By the time I found my outfit again, they were stopped to let the Russians come up to us.

One day a jeep showed up with the driver yelling that the war was over. We fired all our ammunition in the air, then said, "What if the war isn't over? We have nothing to defend ourselves with!"

Those of us who wanted to were driven to Buchenwald concentration camp. When the United States liberated the camp, the dead were piled in the courtyard as high as a building.

One good thing happened to me then. The Army looked for an ex-MP who could speak German. I was the only one who fit. The job was to be chief of police (of a German territory). That's a good job for a guy who had made it all the way to Pfc.

After that we went to a prison in France to guard Americans who had committed felonies. I had a huge carrot and stick. Do your time right and you could get out in six months a free man. Or you could screw up and serve 20 years on Leavenworth. Oddly enough, a lot of fellows chose the latter.

Josh Grossberg

Richard Gerry Dingman – Korea

Richard Gerry Dingman keeps a display case in his home lined with some of the honors he's earned as a military airman. There are six medals, a Silver Star, three Legion of Merit awards, a Distinguished Flying Cross, and honors from the presidents of Korea and the United States.

He enlisted too late to see any action in World War II, but was involved in one of the last actions of he Korean conflict. After a 35-year military that included 1,500 hours of combat flying time, including a tour in Vietnam, the Air Force colonel retired in 1980. He now gives flying lessons.

For all his medals, Dingman is most grateful for one he never received.

The North Koreans and the Chinese communists had 60,000 troops all ready to go through the battle line and take out the South Korean divisions.

The South Korean troops were not that experienced and usually got eaten up pretty bad by the North because they'd been doing a lot of training. Their plan was to punch a big hole in the South, make a big incursion and say, "OK, now we'll make a truce."

One afternoon we went for a briefing. We were told it was top secret. Our plan was to have one bomb wing – 24 planes – fly across at an angle. A surface burst would blow them out of their foxholes and an air burst would blow them back in.

In 15 minutes, the next bomb wing came across and, 15 minutes later, another one. We totally pattern bombed the area. The report after the mission was 90 percent of the troops were disabled or eliminated. They weren't doing any combat after that.

In 1971, I was at the War College and talked to someone. They were driving through this area we had bombed. They had a whole lot of Army trucks loaded with unslaked lime. And guys were standing there shoveling it all over the ground. There was nothing but hamburger and body parts there. The guys driving up there were all over the side of the road, leaving their breakfast there. It was a bad scene. But we essentially wiped out five Chinese communist divisions. That was a pretty bad move as far as anybody trying to plan a mission goes.

We never went up without being shot at. We got bounced a lot, but we never had any damage. It was unreal. Thankfully, I don't own a Purple Heart.

Tom Lasser – Vietnam

Tom Lasser knew he wanted to fly helicopters and serve in the military. So, on Dec. 30, 1965 – exactly 30 years to the day after his father signed up – he enlisted. He never left the military. Lasser spent the first part of his career flying for the Army, serving two tours in Vietnam. After returning home in the early 1970s, he joined the National Guard. The lieutenant colonel spent years working as a government liaison.

I flew over a thousand missions in two tours. I was young and single. If I was married, had a family or was older, I wouldn't have volunteered. I got my draft notice halfway through my first tour.

I was shot down once and wounded twice. The first time I was landing a special forces team in front of a 50-caliber machine gun. The crew got wounded, the aircraft crashed. I only had shrapnel. My wounds were the lightest of them all, knock on wood, thank God. I was treated and released. The only reason I spent the night in the hospital was they couldn't get me back to my unit. I was more scared and bloody than hurt.

I had to get back up there. I was young. I didn't feel it affected me as much as I thought, but the next night, I couldn't sleep.

The second time I was wounded was the second night of my second tour. Rockets went off and I got hit on the foot by a piece of shrapnel.

There's a little macho aspect that comes out. You don't want your buddies to think you're a wimp. It was, "Hey I'm going to get up, shave, put on my flight suit and go back out there." But don't get me wrong. I was scared to enough.

The first guy I knew that got killed was buddy of mine. I picked up Stars and Stripes and saw the casualties. I was only in Vietnam for a week and it hit home. I knew this guy. I felt it then, but you can't think about it.

The closest it came to hitting me was the first time I visited the Vietnam Veterans Memorial wall and saw the name of a guy I knew pretty well – Gerry Latini. In flight school they lined us up A to Z. He was the next guy in line. we were roommates. He died right before I got shot down. I hadn't thought about him very much. Some of the stuff you put out of your mind.

One of these days it might sink in, but I just consider myself lucky for surviving two tours – 24 months – in the combat zone.

Milton Herring – Iraq

Milton Herring has seen war from all sides. As a young man in the 1960s, he enlisted in the Air Force, and as a chaplain now provides guidance at a Veterans Center.

Herring also spent time in the Iraq conflict, where he used his training to help troops in a mortuary unit burdened with one of the most emotional jobs in the military: receiving and processing remains of men and women killed in action.

It was very stressful dealing with the death. It was stressful seeing the remains. My job was to provide ministry to the soldiers who worked very professionally, and making sure that what they did honored the fallen. The Marines call their fallen "angels," and it was quite touching to be a part of that. We would call their names and there would be flags presented.

It's a team of several chaplains of different faiths. And I was happy to see there was a great move of God going on there. Kind of a spiritual revival. We had baptisms in the desert. Young men and women were hungry for God in their lives and very receptive to the ministry of chaplains. There were imams there for people of the Muslim faith.

I found it a spiritual oasis in the desert. There were not as many distractions as in the states and it gave people time to reflect on their spiritual needs. And, of course, there was the possibility of imminent danger and death in some cases.

It strengthened my faith because I was challenged to live what I preached in that setting and what I've been preaching all my life about God's provision, and God's protection. It came down to, did you really believe this? I was able to minister to that and to live as an example of the faith and the faith in God.

For some of them, it was the first time away from home in a dangerous situation. There were a lot of unknown factors. But they found a way to keep themselves encouraged and believe in the leadership and did their jobs.

I don't know how it affected me. It's still emotional for me to reflect on those times. It was a great honor to be able to serve my country in that way.

The time of separation was the most difficult part, being separated from my wife and children. But what helped was knowing that all of us who were deployed were making the same sacrifice.

I love this country and I'm proud and honored to have been able to serve and make some contribution to give back. America is not perfect by any stretch of the imagination, but, all in all, it gets some things quite well.

Mike Biernetzky – Kuwait

When Mike Biernetzky joined the Marines in 1985, he hardly knew where Kuwait was. But he quickly learned about Middle East politics after Iraq invaded the small emirate in 1990.

Biernetzky, an acupuncturist and expert in Eastern medicine, found himself training under a hot Saudi Arabian sun to prepare for Desert Storm. He carried books about Chinese philosophy and a satchel of Chinese herbs with him. During his eight years in the service, he also served in Somalia and Central America.

We were on a cruise to Canada to conduct joint training with the Canadian marines. As we were heading to

Vancouver, they turned us around. I remember watching the news on the ship that Iraq had invaded Kuwait and I thought, "Where the heck is Kuwait? And who cares?" Apparently we did.

I can honestly say that I never had any fear in combat. I'm not a bad person, I never screwed anybody over in the past. If I got killed, nobody would be happy, but this is what we trained for. We were just doing our job.

We the ground war kicked off, we went all the way into Kuwait City. It was unbelievable the destruction outside the city by the Iraqis. We'd see them fleeing south along some highway and they were all driving Mercedes and Beemers and wearing UCLA sweatshirts.

The Iraqis looked like that had performed demolition derbies in new Maseratis and Mercedes. They were littered all over the place.

The Iraqis had trenches everywhere. The tanks would take out any heavy guns they had and we would jump into the trenches and clean them out.

We got fired on a few times. One time, we were entirely unprepared. We had rolled into this position around midnight and had to dig a hole. When dawn started breaking, there was so much fog, you couldn't see.

As it started clearing, they told us to fill in our holes, which I knew was a mistake. We filled in the holes, and out of nowhere, we got hit upon.

Rounds all over the place. I ran around getting a head count of my squad, making sure everything was cool. And then I hit the deck and tried to become sand. "I'm sand. I'm not here."

Never in a million years would I have expected for there to be a war. But when you join, you know anything can happen. I loved being a Marine. A day hasn't gone by that I haven't missed it.

Invisible Wounds

(First published in 2006)

They are our most honored and our most scorned. They put their lives on the line to serve their country, but had trouble reacquainting themselves with the world they left behind.

They are veterans and they are homeless. They are veterans and they are criminals.

They are people like Robert Hearns of Inglewood, Calif. After serving in the Air Force during the Vietnam era, Hearns spent years living on the streets and in prison.

They are people like Michael Jackson, 45, who says he turned to drink and drugs after he left the Army in the early 1980s.

But they are also people like Matt Davison, who drives thousands of miles every month to help fellow veterans who have fallen on hard times.

"I felt really bad how the Vietnam vets were treated when they returned to this country," he said. "I wanted to find a way to help them back. I wanted to try to find a way to help those who were hurting. Those wounds are never visible, but I know they happen. And they're out there."

Davison runs the Incarcerated Veterans Transition Program at Joint Efforts, a social service center. He and a team of specialists work with men and women in four federal prisons to provide counseling, job training and, when the prisoners are freed, help them find work, housing or any other assistance they need.

The program is one of four in the country funded by the Department of Labor and the Department of Veterans Affairs.

According to the National Coalition of Homeless Veterans, there are more than 200,000 homeless veterans, and 225,000 more serving time in prison.

The reason for the high numbers has to do with young people not learning how to handle life outside of the military, said Ralph Berman, an outreach specialist with the program.

"I'm a Vietnam vet," he said. "From what I saw, most people were young and never learned emotional and social skills. We were cared for. It was an adventure. But the support didn't match the need. We missed out on what everybody did. We had no job training, no education and a desire for adrenaline."

The incarcerated program evolved out of a homeless outreach program that Davison started at Joint Efforts in the early 2000s.

Hearns said the program helped turned his life around.

"I didn't care if I went back to the pen or died," he said. "I was on drugs and not caring about myself."

Hearns had a job, but both his sister and mother became ill and he went on a downward spiral.

"I was spiritually broken," he said. "I had a negative outlook on life."

After losing his job, he started getting into drugs. When his mother died, he found himself living on the streets.

"People think vets have it made in life," he said. "But that's a myth."

When he met the folks at Joint Efforts, however, things began to change.

"They personally drove me to the mission," he said. "They didn't have to do that. They are my guardian angels. I don't think I would have made it without them."

Now sober for more than three years, Hearns is studying to become a substance abuse counselor.

"Today I have a car that's paid for," he said. "I even have a credit card. It took me 54 years on this Earth to get one."

Jackson said his problems with drugs and alcohol started

when he joined the Army after high school. He was discharged after a drunken driving episode.

His downward spiral continued until he was living on the streets.

After stints in county jail for drug possession, he decided to turn his life around. He had met Davison at a Veterans Affairs hospital and looked him up.

"They got me into a sober living facility my first day," said Jackson, who is taking college classes. "They continue to be a support. I didn't have a lot of people skills."

But the staff said that if there's any credit to be handed out, it's to the veterans who come and ask for help.

"We open the door, but they have to walk through it," said Tonie Chavez, a case manager with the homeless veterans program.

Although far fewer than their male counterparts, there are women who return from military service and wind up in trouble. They have an ally to cater to their special needs, too.

"Being a woman in the man's military, there were barriers for them," said case manager LaTanya Lott.

Davison started helping his fellow veterans after a successful business career. He'd made a good living, and he wanted to do something more with his life.

"I was a creative director for J. Walter Thompson, which is the furthest thing from what I do now," he said. "That pays well, but you come home at the end of the day and you're empty. You haven't touched a life, you've sold toothpaste."

For the veterans, a helping hand can make all the difference in the world.

"They made me feel like I mattered," Hearns said.

Since starting the incarcerated veterans program, Joint Efforts has helped about 300 people find their footing.

"We only know of two people who have been re-incarcerated since we started the program in 2003," Davison said. "We'd like to have zero, but we'll take two."

Funding for the center's homeless program is always an issue. And although the organizers plan to continue as long as they can, money for the incarcerated vet program is hard to come by.

But Davison makes no secret of the fact that as long as he's around, any veteran who needs assistance will find it.

"We don't turn any vets away," he said.

Last Letter Home

(First published in 2001)

Nearing nervous collapse after days of nonstop air attacks by American forces, Imperial Japanese Army Lt. Kumataro Kubota wrote a letter to his pregnant wife from a trench deep in the Marshall Islands.

The Japanese soldier described the horrific things he had seen since his last letter – "hell-like scenes" of men blown to pieces by shrapnel. Two dozen of his fellow soldiers had already been killed and more than double that number injured.

Yet Kubota also wrote of mundane things, like plans for sending his wife soap, handkerchiefs and towels. On that winter day in 1944, he had one wish for himself.

"Today it's Dec. 24 and New Year's Day is coming very soon," he wrote.

"Good day or bad day, we will probably have a great gift of enemy bombing. I just hope I can survive until the end of this year."

Kumataro got his wish; he survived until February, but not long enough to mail the letter.

* * *

He was a 23-year-old untested Marine standing in a field of dead bodies left to bloat and blacken in the sun for several weeks.

But standing there, surrounded by the corpses of 4,000 Japanese soldiers, Tom Jones saw something that caught his eye: A piece of paper scrawled with Japanese writing – a language Jones didn't know – poking out of the shirt pocket of one of the dead nearby.

"I just knew it was probably his last letter home," Jones said.

He picked up the folded pages and stuffed them into his own pocket.

The note wound up in his foot locker, which eventually got lost in the mess of his garage.

The letter remained unread for more than 50 years.

* * *

Now 80 and semi-retired, Jones found his thoughts meandering back to the time he tried so hard not to remember.

With time on his hands and a story he wanted to share, Jones sat down to write a book about his experience during "World War II. The View From My Foxhole" was the result, a firsthand account of wartime hell.

"It took me three years to live and 55 years to forget and two years to write," said Jones, who worked as a copywriter at an advertising agency.

"I knew the letter was there, but I was trying to forget it. Writing was my business. If you're busy, you don't feel like going home to write. I shoved it aside until I retired."

He dug out the foot locker and opened it. There was a vintage Life magazine, yellowed orders of transfer and the letter. It was clear that it had taken several days to compose; the writing on the first few pages was neat and straight. But by the end, after days of hunger and fear, the Japanese characters looked as if they'd been scrawled by a child.

"Each of us is on the verge of nervous breakdown, and what's more, many of our men suffer with dysentery; so they don't look like live men and their faces are blue," the letter read.

By now, Jones had a friend who could translate the missive. Junko Matsumoto was the daughter of a Japanese general who not only deciphered the letter's contents, but helped Jones navigate an international maze and eventually deliver it to its intended destination.

* * *

Jones had a few clues. He knew the soldier's name and the name of his hometown. With Matsumoto's help, he contacted the mayor of Matsayama City, who helped in the search. The quest began in June and they received the answer they were waiting for by the end of July.

Kubota is a fairly common name in Japan – although "not like Suzuki or Sato," Matsumoto said – yet it wasn't long before word reached the Jones home that the family had been located. Kubota's daughter, Chizuko, had married but retained her father's last name and had stayed in the town.

So too did his widow, Yasuko, who was now 82.

The mayor presented Chizuko with the letter at a special ceremony.

She, in turn, gave it to her mother at home so she could read it in private.

"I am so glad to receive my father's letter to my mother while she is still alive," said Chizuko Kubota, 59, to a Japanese newspaper. "This is the best keepsake for us."

Yasuko Kubota told the Jones family that she had been reading the letter over and over again. She said she had no ashes of her husband, but this was almost like getting him back.

The families have yet to meet, but photographs have

been exchanged, and the Kubotas plan a visit.

"I'd really like to meet them," said Tom's wife, Peggy. "It's almost like we have a new family now."

More than her husband, Peggy Jones seems to have taken the episode to heart, perhaps because she knows it could have been her who received a long-lost letter.

"Just looking at the picture makes you want to cry," she said. "The emotions are overwhelming. It's like receiving a message from the past. He was thinking about her at the last moment and now she knows that."

For his part, Jones said he wrote his book to warn about the dangers of war.

"I'm trying to de-glorify war," he said. "There are good guys on both sides."

In the world of soldiers, there are no hard feelings. They know they may be trying to kill each other, but it's not a personal issue, Jones said. After the war, he would have preferred to sit down with a Japanese soldier for a drink than with an American who didn't fight.

"We'd have something to talk about," he said.

Jones feels the same way about Kubota.

"He would have been fun to talk to," he said. "He appeared to be a nice guy, but nice guys are killed in every war, unfortunately."

The Bloodiest Battle

(First published in 1994)

It has been said that Adolf Hitler came within 22 miles of conquering the world. That's the width of the English Channel that separates England and France.

The channel proved too daunting for Hitler, who thought its waters too turbulent to cross. But the allied forces knew they would have to traverse the channel if they were going to conquer Nazi Germany, so preparations for an invasion of the beaches at Normandy began in early 1943.

Officially, the invasion was known as Operation Overlord. Gen. Dwight D. Eisenhower, the allied expeditionary forces' supreme commander, called it the Great Crusade. History remembers it simply as D-Day.

Whatever the name, the events of June 6, 1944, remain the largest amphibious operation in history.

By June of 1944, almost three-million men of the allied forces had assembled in southern England. Supporting them were 16-million tons of supplies, 5,000 ships, 4,000 landing craft and more than 11,000 aircraft.

The invasion had been planned for June 5, but bad weather forced Eisenhower to postpone it for one day.

The beach landing was preceded by a night drop of the 82nd and 101st airborne divisions behind the German coastal defenses.

The first assault troops waded ashore in the early morning of June 6. The hardest fighting took place on Omaha Beach, where American infantrymen encountered mine fields, barbed wire, booby traps and German soldiers firing down on them from fortifications atop steep bluffs overlooking the beach.

Things went better on nearby Utah Beach, but the fighting there was also severe.

All told, 150,000 men took part in the D-Day invasion. Of that number, some 10,000 were killed or wounded.

For the 50th anniversary in 1994, a group of veterans talked about what it was like to be there.

Here are their stories in their own words:

Charles Perman

Charles Perman joined the Army in 1943. He didn't like

to talk about his experiences during the war, especially the six months he spent as a prisoner of war. But the onetime certified public accountant kept the telegram the Army sent to his wife informing her that he was missing in action. And next to the telegram, in a framed box, he kept the pen his wife gave him before he shipped overseas. He refused to give it up while he was held captive, even though he could have bartered it for food. When he was liberated, he was carried out on a stretcher.

We trained out in the desert for about nine months before we went over to England. From there, we boarded a ship and I was picked to be part of the landing party. I was a battery clerk, not a rifleman. I had experience firing the M1 and being tested crawling under fire, but an infantryman is different from a battery clerk, who basically does clerical work.

I had a rifle over my shoulder and was carrying a typewriter in my other hand and I had to climb down a 30-foot rope ladder, which I had never done before. I damn near fell, but I got down.

Like everything else in life, you got through it. It wasn't an act of bravery. It wasn't an act of special courage. It wasn't a heroic act. It was just at that point you come out with your recorder and pencils and paper and you do your job.

When we hit the water, the captain was making an exit and he got shot right between the bars on his helmet and it killed him right there. We exited on his body. That was tough. At that point, your concern wasn't stepping on a body, it was getting ashore under fire.

You don't think of yourself as a hero.

You have a job you're trained to do and if something bad happens to you, then that's fate.

Richard Hayes

Richard Hayes, a guard at Eisenhower's headquarters in England, knew something big was in the works when he saw maps pinned to the wall with arrows pointing across the English Channel.

Whatever it was, Hayes wanted to be part of it.

D-Day was his first big campaign, but not his last. He received two Bronze Stars and was among the first Americans to enter the Buchenwald death camp in Germany.

He blamed his lifelong hearing problems on the terrible din that day at Utah Beach.

I got tired of standing around in a white uniform and saluting officers. I wanted to see some action, so I volunteered for the infantry.

D-Day was a rainy and dismal day, and the channel was choppy. Excitement ran high and we were all scared, but in a way, we all felt invincible when we saw this big armada that was backing us up. We thought this should be a breeze, easy going. We were carrying heavy field equipment, and we secretly threw our gas masks away to lighten our load.

As we got near the beach, we piled into landing craft like sardines. We hit a sand bar, not the beach itself. There was plenty of water ahead of us, but it was too late. We had to go holding our M1s above our heads. In some places, we were chest deep in the water. The enemy gunfire was shooting up water spouts between the boats. We were all concerned about just getting ourselves to shore.

I didn't get to do too much shooting because we were racing across the beach. A lot of GI Joes would hit the beach and start firing at an unseen enemy. The fire and confusion was all around us.

One of the GIs next to me got it pretty bad, so I pulled him into a shallow ditch. But a voice kept yelling at us, "Keep going, keep going."

I saw some bodies lying around, but we had to keep on going. An infantryman is in his own little world, thinking of himself. I've been very fortunate. I've had cuts, bruises, frozen feet, but you didn't get a Purple Heart for those. I was luckier than most. I didn't have a bullet with my name on it.

My 7-year-old grandson is starting to ask questions. He has a "Star Wars" imagination. He asked me if I fought with lasers. I said no, it wasn't that kind of war. It was a bloody and dirty war.

Vernon Grosscup

From the window of his high-rise apartment, Vernon Grosscup had a spectacular view of Santa Monica Beach. It was a view that Grosscup said looked similar to the beach at Normandy. By the time he got there to fight on D-Day, Grosscup had already been in several battles, including the invasions of North Africa and Sicily. Among the decorations the truck driver received were three Bronze Stars. He served in the Army for four years, two months and 14 days.

We were on the small landing craft, which holds a small company of men. Some of us got seasick pretty horrible. We landed on Omaha Beach around 11 a.m. By that time, there wasn't much going on, just a few shells coming in.

One of the things that got me more than anything else was when we got off the ship, there was one of our dead soldiers on the beach. He had real red hair and he was just laying in the beach looking up at the sky. I often wondered who he was and what happened to him.

Things really weren't that bad. I saw worse in Africa. I was already a veteran. But you can't get over the fear; it's there all the time. The worse thing is the incoming shells. They scare you more than anything else

The next morning we happened to be on a spot that was quiet and peaceful. We were in an open field and there was a beautiful blue sky. There were a dozen cows eating the grass and I thought, "My God, you'd never know there was a war going on." Those cows were so contented.

I loved it when we liberated French towns. The people would come out and scream, "Vive l'Amerique, vive l'Amerique." It made you feel good. They gave us wine. They'd hold up their babies. Young girls would kiss you. It almost made you feel like a hero. I thought, this is worth fighting for.

They say you never hear the shell that hits you, and I never heard it. A fragment of a shell went through the side of my helmet and hit me in the side of the head. They took it out and sent me back to the battle the next day.

It's plain luck whether you get killed or not. All the praying in the world wouldn't do you a bit of good if you're in the wrong place at the wrong time. I've had people killed who were only a few feet away, and I survived.

A lot of guys got lots more decorations than I did. I'm just happy I lived through it. It's an experience I wouldn't want to go through again, but I wouldn't trade it for a million dollars.

Almon M. Doan

It was Almon M. Doan's biggest regret that it broke his mother's heart when he enlisted in the Army. He received a

Josh Grossberg

Bronze Star and two Purple Hearts in the war. Working with a communications unit, he was with the second wave of men who landed on Omaha Beach.

When we left England, we left in the twilight, and I stood out on the ship. There were a lot of men around, but I was by myself and I thought this might be the last time I ever see anything behind me ever again.

The beach was a good 300 yards of nothing, but sand and obstacles. We had to go in at 5 in the morning because the low tide would expose all the traps.

The radios were heavy and some of them got wet and didn't work. Unfortunately, if the man carrying the radio got killed, the radio would be left floating in the saltwater. Ours made it to the retraining wall where we were told to hold.

Some of the guys were wounded bad. This one engineer got hit, and I went back and picked him up and was pulling him and got shot in the back. That took me out of action.

I was 20 years old and I was scared. The biggest pain I had was being scared. The magnitude of what was going on just numbed you so you were just bewildered. I couldn't do anything and that made me more bewildered and more scared.

All day I lay on the beach and was evacuated later that evening and was operated on. I was young and there was no reason I couldn't heal fast. I have to be honest, if I had had my way, that would have been the end of it right there, but that wasn't the way they worked it, so I went back to the outfit.

The hardest part of being wounded was knowing the telegram would be going to my parents.

There were so many men shot doing what I did. They'd run out and get these fellas and bring them back. I remember one general came right up alongside me and said you either get up off the beach or you die here. I'm telling you, that got the men going.

Later, they were bringing prisoners back. The German prisoners were old men and young boys. That had a profound effect on me as a 20-year-old being wounded and lying there. All we had been seeing and hearing and feeling was the enemy's nonpresence. We were feeling everything, but it didn't have an association with another person like myself. And then to see those men who were just like me. They were human just like me. They just had on different uniforms. I was too scared and hurt to have any animosity toward them.

John Bersinger

John Bersinger's home was just down the street from the plant where B-17 bombers were built. Bersinger flew one of the "Flying Fortresses" in two bomber missions on D-Day. But most of his work was completed in the months before, when he helped cripple Germany's air power.

He still carried the bullets in his shoulder from enemy fire he received during the first of his 32 missions. The onetime mortgage banker received a Purple Heart, Distinguished Flying Cross and four Flying Medals.

It was unbelievable. There was good weather and there were boats as far as you could see. They were like flies creeping across the channel.

Eisenhower's last encouraging words before the push, the most important thing he said to those guys was, "On the morning of D-Day, when you look up and see an airplane, it will be a friendly one."

In other words, we had broken the back of the German air force. Our guys would never have gotten to the French coast if they had been under heavy German air attacks. But they could forget about the air because the Germans weren't there.

January of 1944 was the dividing point of the war. Before that, the Germans controlled the air. In one mission, 244 German fighters were destroyed and that was viewed, in retrospect, as the day the war changed. From then on, we controlled the air. That is the main reason the fellas invading Normandy didn't have to worry about what was in the sky.

On D-Day, our group hit two targets. One was close to the beachhead where the Germans were dug in pretty well. The second was a little French village inland about 20 miles. We did all we could to stop the opposition for the guys who were landing on Omaha Beach. It was so close to England, which is why we could fly two missions.

We were at 12,000 feet, which was low altitude. The lower the altitude, the greater the accuracy.

When we took off at dawn, there was this tremendous

flotilla going across the channel. We would open our bomb-bay doors on the southern coast of England because it was only 25 miles and we covered that in nothing flat. Occasionally, the bomb-bay doors and bomb release mechanism would malfunction. I saw two planes drop their whole load, which must have been 50 bombs, right down into the channel where our guys were. I couldn't see if they hit anything. It makes you sick in the stomach, but those things happen. That's war.

We went to our 50th high school reunion in 1988. We were of the vintage that was ripe for World War II. The thing that really hit me was so many of those guys died at the age of 20 and 21, and here we were old fossils going to our 50th reunion. I couldn't help but think of those fellas that never had a shot of doing anything. But that's what makes for a war, I guess.

Joseph Ductor

Joseph Ductor kept some of the mementos from his days in the war: a German helmet and field glasses, an Italian dagger, an English knife. Trained in amphibious landings, Ductor was among the first to land on Utah Beach. By then, he had already been battle-tested in campaigns in North Africa and Italy.

I was fortunate. We landed on the wrong beach, about a half mile away from where we were supposed to, which was good. The poor guys on Omaha Beach really got it.

In retrospect, I think it was a mistake to land on Omaha. They shouldn't have gone up the cliffs. I have a friend who got out alive, but he got hurt and went crazy.

We were on the beach for a while and I don't remember sleeping. I know I didn't sleep for a couple of days. I must have dozed off somewhere. We were there for a week.

The beach was all sandy. A lot of people could have stayed alive, but they were in foxholes that were too deep. They should be about 12 inches deep, but they dug some that were several feet deep. They were caved in.

The son of Theodore Roosevelt was there. He wanted to go on the invasion. He was in his 50s. He turned around and told our colonel, "You take care of the beach." One week later, he died of a heart attack. That's the way he probably wanted to go.

About that time I could realize this war is not going to last very long. We knew the end was coming. And it did.

That evening, they sent reinforcements over and they told our unit they were going to be dropping right above us. The problem is not everybody else knew. Some of our own troops were shooting at their own planes. I was hollering, but nobody could hear you with all that going on. You look back on it. That's war, isn't it? Those things happen and they still happen. Mistakes are bound to happen. How can war be perfect? It would be a beautiful game.

As long as you came back alive, it would be a beautiful game.

Dr. William Coleman.

Dr. William Coleman joined the Army a week before he received his bachelor's degree in 1942. He was new to his battalion when it landed on Omaha Beach, where he served as a forward observer. He received a Bronze Star and a Purple Heart.

Since our guns were mounted on tank chassis, we were able to get our guns into the beach area despite the high waters. The German guns were firing at us from the pillboxes that had not been destroyed, which is why there was a lot of death.

I was a newcomer to that battalion. I was placed on a ship that was not scheduled to land until two hours after the invasion, but because of losses, I did not get ashore until eight hours later. I was on a landing craft watching what was going on from several miles out. A lot of people were half drowned. I could see that stuff, but there wasn't much I could do.

I'm very grateful to the officers who had been in combat who were able to keep me from getting into trouble.

Once we got off the cliffs, the Germans were pretty much reserve types and old-timers, not front-line troops, and they didn't do too much damage.

There were times I was out there as a forward observer, out ahead of the people to our right and left, and that's when we could see some Germans. They were more concerned about saving their own skins. Radar was still not around, and I was directing the fire by being in a forward position.

I didn't experience anyone close to me injured, although as I climbed up the steep cliffs, I did run into a fellow I knew in high school. I think he called my name. I went over and saw him. It was more meaningful to me because these guys in the 62nd and I had gotten acquainted, but we weren't close buddies. We hadn't had the bonding that occurs when you go through fire or through hell with someone.

This guy had been seriously wounded and died after I saw him. I won't say he was my closest buddy, but we knew each other, played ball with each other.

A Day of Infamy

(First published in 2001)

Edward Kronberger doesn't usually spend much time thinking about Pearl Harbor.

That was a long time ago, he says, and he was just a kid. But Kronberger recently found himself leafing through a tattered scrapbook filled with yellowed news clippings and mementos."For years I didn't think about it," he says. "Now guys are coming out of the woodwork. Guys are getting old and sentimental."Even though he's moved on, the walls of the study in his home are lined with pictures of ships and men in sailor uniforms – his dad and three brothers all served in the Navy. He's 81 now, but he'll never forget that day. He spent early morning Dec. 7, 1941, on overnight watch, then he went below deck for some sleep. At 4 a.m. he rested his head under a locker to keep the light from his eyes and fell asleep. The first explosion woke him with a start.

"I jumped up and hit that locker with my head," he says. "I heard something, but I didn't know what it was. I was still asleep."

A swaggering 21-year-old who liked to drink and have a little fun, he was on the USS West Virginia. His dad, Sam, and brother, Robert, were somewhere on the ship, too, but he wouldn't find out their fate for another day. Thinking his ship had been hit by another ship, he stumbled to his battle station and tried to collect some ammunition.

"The magazine was locked, so we stood outside waiting for instructions," he said. "You're in a daze. You don't know what's going on."

He laughs about it now, the confusion, the panic, the mother back home who had no idea if half her family was dead or alive.

"They thought I was dead," he says. "It was a week before my mother found out."

It turns out his brother and father also survived. Hit by at least nine torpedoes, the West Virginia started to sink. Kronberger climbed his way to the top and then made his way to another ship. Over the next few weeks, 67 bodies were recovered.

"We took a bomb hit from above, but it didn't go off," he says. "But the pressure blew a hatch open and killed four or five guys."

When he thinks about his friends who died, he grows quiet and stares off into space for a few seconds. His unwavering voice suddenly cracks. But before he lets the feeling overcome him, he jumps from his chair and pours himself another cup of coffee from the chrome percolator in his tidy kitchen.

It's the details that stick in his mind. He remembers being hungry and, with no ammunition to fight with, he made a bologna sandwich and then found a car and drove to a nearby air base.

"I bought a brand new pair of tailor-made blues," he says. "I lost them. That made me mad."

And, though he doesn't dwell on it, he still holds anger at Japan for staging the attack.

"I'm still mad in a way," he says. "I have a lot of Japanese friends, but they're American. The Japanese never apologized. I guess they never will."

Kronberger stayed in the Navy until 1960 and then worked at a shipyard. He married and raised two children. And like he says, he didn't spend too much time thinking about Pearl Harbor.

"We had other things to do," he says. "We led a good life, I guess. Pearl Harbor didn't bother me too much. I was a young guy. I didn't know too much."

The Kiss

(First published in 2005)

After years of fighting, thousands of deaths and hundreds of battles, the image that came to symbolize the end of World War II was something as simple as a single kiss.

But not just any kiss. When Edith Shain stepped off a New York subway 60 that day, she smooched her way into history.

"It was a very long kiss," she recalled, "very long. I figured he deserved it."

It was Aug. 15, 1945. Japan had just surrendered to Allied forces. World War II had finally come to an end. And Shain, still wearing her white nurse's uniform, wanted to celebrate.

"As soon as we heard the war was over, everybody went to Times Square," she said.

Famed Life magazine photographer Alfred Eisenstaedt was there, too. On the prowl for an image that would represent the historic moment, he happened to catch Shain just as she was swooped into the arms of a passing sailor.

"It was the end of the war, kiddo," she said. "It was a great time. All the women were grabbed."

Thirteen days later the image appeared in Life and was immediately recognized as a classic.

It was a kiss that would not only come to symbolize America's victory in World War II, but also the country's sense of unbridled optimism for the future.

"It's a lyrical picture," Shain said. "It's exquisitely designed. It was the end of the war and it was pure heaven. There was so much energy, such love. And not only the end, but the beginning of everything. And I never told anyone except my girlfriend. I was too embarrassed. I didn't want to talk about it."

Many women – and dozens of men – have claimed to be the kissers, but Shain eventually came forward in 1980. While the magazine won't confirm her identity, she received Eisenstaedt's seal of approval when the two finally met and became friends.

"He saw my legs and that was it," she said. "He knew my size. I guess that made an impression."

She may be the most famous kisser in history, but the

only clue to her identity in her West Los Angeles home is a watch she wears with her likeness – back arched, right leg bent at the knee, lips locked with a strange man in a sailor suit – on the dial.

She mostly keeps the photo hidden, but Shain is familiar to scores of aspiring artists. For years, she donned her famous white outfit and posed for students at a local adult school.

She was a student of artist George Gardiner when the two became friends. He asked her to pose for him after that. Gardiner was a young man when the war ended, but he has a clear memory of seeing Shain.

"I remember the picture," he said. "It was electrifying. That picture caught America at its moment of joy. It symbolized everything, the joy of victory, but not vindictively."

Like the photo of men raising the flag on Iwo Jima, Gardiner said the picture of the kiss has become an American icon.

"The dark uniform of the Navy, the white dress of this nurse. The pose is melodramatic. When a student found out who she was, they said, 'Why, you're a national treasure.' "

The mother of three spent years working as a teacher. Most of her neighbors don't know about her brush with fame but, when they find out, they're usually amazed.

"They say, 'Oh my God,' " she said. "They get so excited. It's amazing how excited people get."

The afternoon he snapped it, Eisenstaedt had been

following a sailor on a kissing spree, taking pictures furiously.

"Then suddenly, in a flash, I saw something white being grabbed," he said before his death in 1995. "I turned around and clicked the moment the sailor kissed the nurse.

"People tell me that when I am in heaven they will remember this picture."

Since the day it was taken, the picture has been reprinted on purses and mouse pads. It's been parodied on "The Simpsons" and the cover of The New Yorker magazine.

Along the way, it's become the most reproduced picture in the history of Life magazine and Shain occasionally gets it in the mail as part of a subscription come-on. On Thursday, she traveled to New York for the unveiling of a statue that re-creates the moment.

"Perhaps never in history has a photographer been able to freeze a moment that is, once the developing fluid has been brushed away, so instantly iconic and representational of something 'other' than Alfred Eisenstaedt did when he captured that sailor kissing that nurse 60 years ago," said Bob Sullivan, Life's deputy managing editor.

"The subjects are anonymous, yet they are all of us. Or, at least, they are all Americans at that point in time, with the war over, the present thrilling and the future boundless."

At least 25 men have claimed to be the sailor, but Shain said she can't be sure which one is correct. She identified one man and posed with him 10 years ago, but she's since changed her mind.

"A lot of people have told me the same thing," she said. "They all have their stories. In the heat of what happened, there were all kinds of photographers around."

The latest candidate is George Mendonsa, a retired fisherman from Rhode Island. To bolster his claim, a team of researchers from the Naval War College ran his image through a computer to see if it matched the head in the picture. Apparently it did.

But Shain said she couldn't possibly be expected to remember what he looked like.

"When you're being kissed," she said, "you close your eyes."

An Unlikely Spy

(First published in 2003)

After all these years, Marthe Cohn can still see his face, still hear his words. She was 24 at the time and listening as a Nazi soldier recounted some exploits.

"He was raving about how many Jews he had killed," she said. "He said he could smell a Jew a mile away. I was sitting right next to him."

That Cohn herself was Jewish never dawned on the man. Who would ever expect this petite wisp of a young woman – standing less than 5 feet tall – would have dared sneak into Nazi Germany while any sane Jew would have done anything to get out?

"You want to throw up, but you keep smiling," she said

of the encounter.

For three harrowing weeks, Cohn wandered alone into enemy territory to help the French Army gain the upper hand.

It's a story so remarkable, in fact, that Cohn waited years to write a book of her experience. She doubted anybody would ever believe her. Not even her two sons knew about her adventure until a few years ago when the French government awarded her one of its highest honors, the Medaille Militaire.

"I never talked about it," she said from the living room of her handsome home. "I thought people would look at me and say 'Yeah, sure.'"

The book, "Behind Enemy Lines," recounts Cohn's life from innocent girl to hardened spy and beyond. And she remembers it all in startling detail – names, times, dates. It's all there.

Cohn draws an imaginary map of Europe with her finger on the top of her dining room table. Here is where she grew up. Here is where her family had to flee when the Nazis invaded France. And here is the border where she tried to elude guards before she was able to make it into Germany. Fluent in the language, she pretended to have escaped from the French. She was knee deep in snow, but unable to wear warm clothing for fear she'd blow her cover.

"I tried 13, 14 times to cross the front," she said. "If you're trained to do it, you do it. It took me several hours and I was terrified. I finally made it and said, 'Heil Hitler.'"

For the next few weeks, she traveled around, looking for valuable information. A trained nurse, she was able to travel fairly freely. In her pocket, she carried the picture of a man she claimed was her fiancé. In fact, he was a German locked away in a French prison. There were a few close calls, like when a woman looked her right in the eye and asked if she was a spy.

"I started laughing and said no," Cohn said. "She started laughing, too."

But there were victories, like when Germans, fleeing the advancing French, confided in her by revealing the location of troops and military equipment that stood ready to fend off the Allied forces.

She was born Marthe Hoffnung on April 20, 1920, in the French city of Metz, which is close to Germany. She learned to speak German from her parents. It was the only language they knew.

The early years were largely uneventful. She was a headstrong girl who loved spending time with her brothers and sisters. But as the dark clouds of war began forming, her family was forced to move to a city deeper inside France.

But after the Nazis took away one of her sisters and killed her fiancé, Cohn decided she wanted to join the army. The problem was, the army didn't want her. As a young woman, she wasn't taken seriously. But when an official learned she could speak perfect German, he recruited her to work as a spy.

Once she was behind the border, she knew no one would be able to help her if she were caught.

"A challenge was something I had to accept," she said. "That was my nature."

It hardly seems possible that this woman with the soft French accent infiltrated one of the most brutal regimes in history. With her easy smile and inquisitive manner, she seems more like the proud grandmother of a 10-year-old girl than a master of espionage.

In the foreword to the book, she notes how surprised her sons were to learn of her history. When told of her exploits, their reaction was "She was just our mom."

And she still doesn't understand what all the fuss is about.

"It was normal for me," she said. "Everything depends on what's going on."

Her husband, Major L. Cohn, had heard some of the stories, but never heard the whole thing before. They were married in 1956.

"Sure I'm proud," he said. "She's very modest about it. I never knew the totality of what occurred. She did amazing things."

The war produced other heroes, but not many, said Rabbi Marvin Hier, dean of the Simon Wiesenthal Center in West Los Angeles.

"She was there all alone," he said. "She had the courage to do that. This was rare. She makes light of it, but her actions were extraordinary. To act as a spy and be caught by a regime as ruthless as the Nazis, she knew what was waiting for her."

Hier said Cohn made such a good spy because she was so unassuming.

"She hardly fit the role," he said. "I could see how she fooled the Nazis. She was very low key and very determined to play that role. She doesn't want to make a big deal about it, but a big deal should be made. It deserved to be documented, not only for those who knew her, but for those who never met her."

And also, perhaps for those who were left behind. In addition to a picture of a young Cohn in a nursing uniform, the cover of the book includes a picture of her sister Stephanie, whom Cohn never saw again after she was hauled off by the Nazis.

"I think about her all the time," Cohn said. "Now she's on the cover of a book, and she'll be seen by thousands of people."

Cohn doesn't dwell on the past, but she does think about it. And sometimes after discussing those days, she has trouble sleeping.

"It's in my brain," she said. "I'll never forget it."

After the war, Cohn served in Vietnam with the French Army. Eventually, she met and married an American, emigrating in 1956 to the United States.

Cohn has a mischievous smile. All those memories are still there, but life is to be enjoyed.

"I fought the Germans so I have no reason to feel bad,"

she said. "You cannot let events get you down. You have to live. It's in my genes."

Sometimes even Cohn betrays a little incredulity at the life she's led.

"I thought spies were tall and gorgeous women," she said. "I was a very unlikely spy."

Raising the Flag

Part 1
(First published in 2006)

Martin Dews knows something nobody else knows. Virtually anybody who can verify his story is dead, but Dews talks about it in tantalizing detail. He can still touch the ground, see the smoke, smell the sulfur in the air.

As Dews tells it, he was among the handful of men who helped plant an American flag on the tiny Pacific island of Iwo Jima near the end of World War II. He wasn't at the second flag-raising on Mount Suribachi, which became one of the most iconic images of the 20th century, but he said he was on hand when a smaller flag was unfurled nearby just a few hours earlier Feb. 23, 1945.

Whether or not the 82-year-old is the only surviving person to participate in the historic flag-raisings is unknown. But he could be.

It's a memory he doesn't want, he said, but it's been following him for more than 60 years and he's finally ready for some recognition.

"I didn't know it would be famous," Dews said.

With the release of Clint Eastwood's movie "Flags of Our Fathers,", Iwo Jima has again entered the public's consciousness. The movie is based on the book of the same name by James Bradley and Ron Powers. Bradley is the son of John Bradley, a Navy corpsman who participated in the second flag-raising.

Fought between the United States and Japanese, the battle for Iwo Jima was one of the bloodiest in the war – about 20,000 Japanese troops were killed and nearly 7,000 American fighters were lost.

"The first day of the invasion, the sands ran red with our blood," Dews wrote in a journal he recently started. "It was like death was spitting at us."

The fighting would continue for months, but Americans quickly took control of Mount Suribachi, the island's highest point. It was the first piece of Japanese soil captured, and American leaders wanted to send a potent message. Dews said he was among the men selected for the chore, even though the battle was still raging on the island.

"We were told to put the flag up," Dews said. "I was

scared to death. I thought I was going to get it."

Dews' story came out when he met a fellow veteran, 61-year-old Craig Gasteiger. When Gasteiger first heard the tale, he wasn't sure if he believed it.

"I didn't know if he was just telling me a story," Gasteiger said. "But the way he described it – if he said he turned left and something was there, there it was. No way anyone would know this who wasn't there."

The son of an FBI agent, Gasteiger researched Dews' claims and compiled documents to back it up. The two are now trying to get Dews a Purple Heart for an injury he said he received on his way down from the mountain.

This is Dews' story:

The 19-year-old Army private left Hawaii in the beginning of January with a contingent of Marines and reached Iwo Jima about six weeks later.

"I don't know how many times guys told me the Army wasn't on Iwo Jima," he said. "I don't understand how somebody can tell me I wasn't there. They don't know what the hell happened."

During the trip, he became friends with some of the men who would become immortalized in stamps, coins, statues and movies. Among them were Franklin Sousley, who died in combat a month later. ("Frankie was a country boy with a Southern accent who loved hunting.") And Ira Hayes, who died in 1955. ("A serious sort, hated to be called Chief, drank hard to forget at times, but a good guy to be in combat with.")

The team landed on the island Feb. 19. The fighting was fierce.

"We were receiving fire from up on Suribachi and other encampments behind us in hidden bunkers in the central section of the island."

On the fourth day, word came that a group of men were to plant a flag on the top of the hill.

"(It) would hopefully raise the morale of any of the battle-strapped Marines who could see it from anywhere on the island or at sea around Iwo Jima," Dews said. "We all needed something. It was a bloodbath. We were kids being told to be men. Many times we heard the dying calling out for their mommas."

By sunup, the group was inching its way to the top of the treacherous plateau at the top of the 546-foot high hill.

"We started up this thing," Dews said. "There was gunfire everywhere."

The island was pocked with caves and hiding places. One of the first things Dews saw was a hospital burrowed inside the hill.

"It was the most modern hospital I had ever seen," Dews said. "What we found was every patient was shot to death. The Japanese didn't want them to be captured. It was hot, dry and dusty, smelling like sulfur. It was a steep, hard climb. We took every step cautiously."

Near the top, a mortar round exploded, killing a Marine.

"This heightened our emotions about getting the job done," he said. "Get the flag up and get out of there. There was debris from a small, bomb-flattened structure and surprising lengths of pipe."

The sergeant told one of the men, Rene Gagnon (who died in 1979) to tie the flag to the pipe.

"One of the Marines pulled out a thick cord and tied the top of the flag to the pole. We found some twine-like material and tied the bottom of the flag."

The men then gathered rocks and pieces of concrete for a base.

"I held the bottom of the pole with my rifle by my knees," Dews said. "The rest raised the pole with the flag blowing in the stiff breeze."

There's a picture of the first flag-raising, but Dews said his face is obscured by another man.

Pointing to a hand holding the pole, he said, "That's me."

Over the years, however, other names have been attached to the hidden man in the picture.

Nine men ventured to the top of the hill that morning. One was killed on the way up and another on the way down.

Near the bottom of the hill, Dews said he was ambushed by a Japanese soldier and hit in the shoulder with a bayonet. The attack broke his collarbone, so he didn't make the return trip a few hours later when commanders decided they wanted to raise a bigger flag.

That's when Associated Press photographer Joe Rosenthal took the famous "Raising the Flag on Iwo Jima." The remaining six men who made the second trip became famous within days and Rosenthal would win the Pulitzer Prize for his effort. He died in August.

But Dews was happy not to make the trek again.

"No one was looking forward to being on top of the mount," he said. "But it was just another job that had to be done."

Gasteiger helped Dews apply for a Purple Heart. Officials are investigating his story, but a fire in 1973 destroyed many Army records and his may not be found, said Eddie Kimes, a national service officer with the Military Order of the Purple Heart. Nonetheless, he found Dews' story compelling.

"There is credibility to his story," Kimes said. "I couldn't find any historical facts with his name, but it seems to be a legitimate story. We're hoping some clerks will dig up some of the facts. Hopefully he'll be awarded the Purple Heart."

Dews' discharge papers at least put him in proximity to Iwo Jima: It notes that he was awarded a Bronze Star and served in the Pacific during World War II. He left the service on Dec. 14, 1945.

After spending the next seven months on the island, the only thing Dews wanted to do was forget it. He got a job two days after he returned home and continued to work in lumberyards until he was 80. Short on money, he said he came forward so he can receive benefits that he thinks are coming to him.

"I went to work," he said. "I worked until 2 1/2 years

ago. Then I thought I could get some money. I deserve it."

If he had his way, Dews wouldn't be talking about Iwo Jima now. He doesn't want fame, only what he feels he deserves.

"When you seen some of the things I seen, you want to forget," he said.

Raising the Flag

Part 2
(First published in 2006)

He faced enemy fire and earned a Bronze Star for heroism.

But now Martin Dews has come under attack from the very men he says he served with.

Last month, Dews told a reporter that he was among the handful of men who helped raise a flag on Iwo Jima. But since the story was published, many Marines – including one who was there – say Dews did not participate in the historic event.

"There's no way this guy was on the mountain with us," said retired Col. Dave Severance, who commanded the company that raised the flag. "His story isn't true."

But the 82-year-old Dews remains adamant.

"I know what I saw," he said. "I was there. I know all this stuff and people say I wasn't there. I don't know why."

According to Dews, he helped plant an American flag on the small Japanese island in the Pacific near the end of World War II. He didn't participate in the second flag-raising, which became one of the most famous images of the war, he said. Instead, Dews said he was on top of Mount Suribachi when the first flag was hoisted a few hours earlier on Feb. 23, 1945.

Dews trembled with anger when told that people don't believe his story.

"Why would I say this if I wasn't there?" he asked.

He said Severance is wrong.

"Severance was not at the top (of the hill)," he said. "Nobody was thinking. It was fast. Everybody was put into duty. How could you keep an itemized list?"

The battle for Iwo Jima was one of the bloodiest in the war – about 20,000 Japanese troops and nearly 7,000 American soldiers were killed.

The October issue of Leatherneck magazine tries to put the matter to rest. In an article titled "Unraveling the Mysteries of the First Flag Raising," the magazine carefully examines photos taken that morning and identifies each of the people involved. But the faces are not easily seen in the black-and-white images, and Dews said the article is mistaken. The magazine identifies one partially hidden man as Phil Ward, but Dews said that's not right.

"They got the wrong names," he said.

The official Marine version accounts for everybody on Mount Suribachi that morning. And none of them was named Martin Dews, said Bob Aquilina, a historian with the Marine Corps' history division.

"(They) have all been identified and they were all Marines," he said.

But Aquilina backed up Dews on one of his most contentious points. For years, Dews said people called him a liar when he told them that Army personnel participated in the early days of the battle.

"Nobody believes the Army was on the island," Dews said. "But there were (Army personnel)."

There was indeed a small contingent of soldiers with the Marine units, Aquilina said.

"There were specific Army elements attached to the Fifth Marine Amphibious Corps," he said. "Specific (Marine) units that ... needed personnel, the Army units filled."

Aquilina doesn't dispute that Dews might have been on the island, only his claim about raising the flag.

"Part of the confusion arises from the fact that there were many individuals on top of Suribachi that day," he said.

"He could well have been there, could well have been up Mount Suribachi. It might well be the way he remembers the facts."

Internet message boards have also taken up Dews' claim, with some people giving him the benefit of the doubt and others saying he invented the tale.

"There are ... cases of men who have been mistreated by doubters of their claims with respect to the flag-raising events who turned out to be telling the God's honest truth," wrote one poster.

"I guess we can add this bit of fiction to the list of the hundreds, if not thousands, of families who claim Gramps, or Unc, or someone they knew raised the flag on Suribachi," wrote another.

Nobody disputes that Rene Gagnon climbed the mountain that morning. His niece Beverly Kawaguchi saw the newspaper article and contacted Dews. After meeting with him, she found his story compelling.

"He seems to have great recollection," said the 62-year-old Kawaguchi. "I don't want to say I don't believe him. He might have been there and God bless him if he was."

Gagnon died in 1979.

Honoring the Dead

(First published in 2007)

When the telephone rings, the old warriors stop talking.

Chito Galvan walks over to the phone, picks it up and speaks softly into the receiver for a few seconds before hanging up.

It was a mortuary calling. A veteran has died and they wanted to know if Galvan and his friends could attend the funeral.

No, Galvan had to tell them, they couldn't. They already promised to be at another cemetery that day.

Galvan returns to his seat and tells his friends about the call. The men of the Veterans of Foreign Wars in Wilmington, Calif., shrug before shaking it off and returning to their chat.

Josh Grossberg

They know the math: More than 1,000 World War II veterans are dying every day. Locally, it's more than they can handle. But they do their best.

For the honor guard from Port of Los Angeles VFW Post 2967, saluting the dead is something they do about twice a week, year round.

A few other posts nearby perform the same service, but the Wilmington branch is known as one of the most professional.

"We are the best known post," said post Cmdr. Howard Hagen. "We're recognized. When people need us, we're here."

Most of the men are in their 70s and 80s now, veterans of World War II and the Korean conflict. Attending memorial services is not a chore they want, but they feel duty-bound to do it. Last year, they performed the ritual at 107 funerals.

"The military wasn't sending them out, so we took it upon ourselves to do this," said 74-year-old Richard Rivas, who served in Korea. "I think we're doing our job as veterans to honor our fallen comrades."

It takes eight men to form a proper honor guard – one chaplain and seven riflemen. But sometimes as few as three will show up if other members are busy. The post has a pool of about 16 men who participate.

"They deserve a military funeral," said Hagen, who also served as the state office chief of staff for the VFW.

A Vietnam veteran, at 64, Hagan is one of the youngest members of the group.

"Sometimes they want us there three or four times a

day," he said.

They don't limit themselves to funerals. There are happy occasions as well. Whether it's the first day of Little League season, a Christmas parade or a Flag Day celebration at an elementary school, they will do their best to show up.

One a recent day, several of them visited a cemetery to place American flags near the graves of those whose headstone indicated military service.

Their bonds are strong. Many of these men grew up together. And after decades of friendship, they feel comfortable enough with each other to joke around at a gravesite while waiting for the funeral procession to arrive.

"We've been together forever," said past Cmdr. Efren Ramirez.

We're like the military," Galvan said. "You develop a bond, a team that works together."

None of them enjoy it, but some of the men have an easier time of their job than others. For Ramirez, being in an honor guard is a mater of pride.

"My grandson said, 'Grandpa, you do a lot of funerals. Doesn't it get depressing?' I said, 'No, mijo. I'm glad to do it. I feel proud to have the opportunity."

But for Rivas, it's more of a burden.

"For me, it's depressing," he said. "I can't do more than a few a week."

And some funerals are harder than others, especially when the deceased is a fellow VFW member.

"It doesn't bother you unless it's someone you know," said Gave Mendoza, a 73-year-old Korea veteran. Then it hurts. I buried a guy I knew since I was 10. It hurt a little bit.

Some of the men no longer drive and rely on their friends or wives to chauffeur them to different locations.

At their age, even carrying a rifle can be an ordeal. The World War II-era M1 rifle they use weighs just over nine pounds and the men can get fatigued holding them. And while they dread funerals on hills because it's more difficult to perform their rituals on slopes, they also laugh about how they sometimes stumble and fall.

Ramirez remembered a time when a funeral at sea left many members feeling queasy.

"Here are the guys trying to fire their rifles and the boat was rocking. I had to hold some of them," he said.

But no matter how frail they are, they try to do their best to show up.

"These guys go the extra mile," Ramirez said. "They don't care if they're limping. We pick them up and keep going."

Finding a new generation of men to perform the duties is not an easy task. Younger veterans tend to shy away from joining groups like the VFW.

"We're hoping we get more in, at least from Vietnam," Hagen said. "But they don't seem to want to be part of the VFW. They have their own groups."

Young veterans think all we do is go into bars and tell old war stories, "Rivas said. "But we don't seem have time to play cards."

At 50, Carlos Murrieta is the baby of the bunch. He

served in the Army in the 1970s and joined the VFW six months ago.

It's like being with a lot of uncles and grandfathers," he said. "I went to a meeting and they asked me if I was interested. I couldn't say no."

Murrieta said that being part of the honor guard has rewards. And he feels proud that he's helping families cope with the loss of a loved one.

"It makes you appreciate life," he said. "Sometimes tears fill my eyes. You can see the emotion and the appreciation it brings the families. It touches deep in your heart. You look at their faces and see them weeping. You see how it affects them. It affects us as well."

Though age is taking its toll on the team, Murrieta is more optimistic than the others about the future of the ritual.

"Everybody is getting old," he said. ""But there's an awakening among the young soldiers. "They're coming around. They're going to have respect and pick up the slack."

Hagen said that when his generation is gone, others will fill the gap.

"It will carry on somehow," he said.

Until that next generation arrives, the men from the Wilmington VFW will carry on with the routine they've performed so many times before.

They always arrive early and wait by the gravesite. Sometimes they wait for hours if a funeral lasts longer than expected. When the grieving families arrive, Ramirez reads a poem and the rest fire their rifles into the air. They then fold an American flag into a tight triangle and hand it to a family member.

They bring a bugle too, but in a nod to modernity, it plays "Taps" electronically while one of them holds the instrument to his mouth.

"Nobody knows how to play them anymore," Hagen said.

Before heading to a funeral, the group gathers at the hall and Hagen retrieves the rifles from a locked safe. Then they perform a few practice drills. Their mood is jovial as they prepare themselves for the chore they're about to do. They stand in the parking lot and make small talk like old friends do before they pile into their cars and caravan to where they're needed.

"Let's hit the road, toad," Rivas said as they started the engines. "Let's get it on."

Homecoming

(First published in 2008)

Logan and Lucas Hede hadn't seen their daddy in eight months, which was practically an eternity for the 2- and 4-year-old brothers.

But as soon as Maj. Mike Hede stepped out of the car, the two boys wrapped their small arms around their father's neck and kissed him.

"I missed them so much," Hede said after greeting a gathering of relatives, including his wife, Lori, at the Naval Marine Corps Reserve Center.

Hede, a member of the 3rd Air Naval Gunfire Liaison Company, was among three dozen military men who returned home from tours of duty in Iraq.

Joining the celebration were members of the local Veterans of Foreign Wars Post 1622 and the post's Women's Auxiliary. Like VFWs around the country, the local chapter has "adopted" troops serving overseas.

"It's important to show them they're not forgotten," said Post Adjutant Doug Perkins.

Sharon Peppy, an auxiliary member, helped organize the event so the homecomings would be as perfect as could be. She knew the Marines wouldn't want to linger at the base – not after being away from their families for so long. But she wanted their loved ones to feel comfortable too, so she and her crew brought cookies, sandwiches and cold drinks. And they decorated the center's walls with balloons and handmade welcome-home signs.

It's part of an ongoing effort for the local VFW.

"Whenever they need us, we're there," Peppy said. "We send care packages, Christmas packages, anything they want, we do."

Lt. Col. Greg Martin, who oversees the base, said even small gestures are greatly appreciated by the troops.

"Our relationship with the VFW is fantastic," he said. "This is the third time I've seen them in the last couple of months."

Seeing their loved ones return home was a relief to family members.

"It's the other end of the spectrum from when they left," said Rene Amy. "I'm glad and relieved. It's nice to see people care. ... It's just a few dozen of them, but the emotion is the same."

The men were expected to show up at 10 a.m., but they got into town on a commercial flight that came in late. By the time they showed up at noon, their loved ones were waiting on the center's front lawn with small flags in their hands.

As they got out of their vehicles, their families erupted into cheers.

For Hede, the next few days will be spent reacquainting himself with his two young sons.

"It sounds like a gosh damn commercial, but we really are going to Disneyland," he said.

He turned to his giggling young boys and said, "You want to go to Mickey Mouse's House?"

And then he gave them another squeeze.

Unknown Soldier

(First published in 2006)

They didn't know much about the man they came to honor: He was 48 years old. He once worked as a mechanic. He was homeless and died alone on the streets.

But David Alan Forbes was also a Marine, and that's all a group of strangers needed to know.

On a Thursday, Forbes was given the honors of a military funeral. At a mortuary in Los Angeles, veterans stood guard by his flag-draped coffin, while Air Force personnel and former Marines sat solemnly in the pews. He was an unknown soldier, but he was their brother.

"As long as he served, he earned this," said Howard Hagen, commander of a nearby Veterans of Foreign Wars post. "He is a veteran, an honorable veteran. He served our country."

For many of the two dozen people in attendance, it would be unthinkable for a fellow military man not to receive his due.

"While I don't know this Marine, I'm here to pay my respects," said Lt. Col. Eric Schnaible of the Los Angeles Air Force Base. "It's a fraternity. Our values are about service. I don't know this man, but he served his nation."

Forbes joined the Marines after graduating from high school in 1975. After the service, he spent 11 years working as mechanic in Tinker Air Force Base in his native Oklahoma.

Then, one day in 1991, he disappeared.

Both his parents died without ever seeing him again. The last time his only sister heard from him was after he was arrested in 1998.

"I think he was so afraid and paranoid," said Christy West from her home in Moore, Okla. "He said it was best this way. And then nothing."

West, who is battling cancer, wasn't healthy enough to make the trip to California. But she was proud that others saw to it that her younger brother received the funeral he deserved.

"I feel so blessed that strangers took it up and gathered together and honored him with a full service," West said.

Forbes died Dec. 16 in Los Angeles. The coroner told his sister that it could take months to determine the cause of death, but no foul play is suspected.

Once she learned about his fate, West contacted a local funeral home.

When they heard about Forbes, they offered their facilities for free.

During his sermon, the Rev. Lance Boloran of the Vermont Avenue Baptist Church didn't say much about Forbes'life. There wasn't much he could say. But he touched upon universal themes.

"(His sister) will never have the opportunity to embrace him or talk to him, but she'll always have the love he felt for her," he said.

As the honor guard marched outside for a final 21-gun salute, Mike C. "Rambo" Miller stood tall and saluted. Miller didn't know Forbes either, but he wore a large patch on the back of his leather jacket that summed up the sentiments of everybody there:

"The nation which forgets its defenders will itself be forgotten," it said.

After the ceremony, Miller rode his motorcycle to Riverside National Cemetery, where Forbes was buried.

"He's a Marine, he's a veteran," said Miller, a retired Marine. "It doesn't matter if I knew him. A veteran is a veteran."

A Different Breed of

Soldier

(First published in 2009)

Ask the people they served with and they'll tell you: The dogs buried at Fort MacArthur in San Pedro served their country with honor, bravery and dignity.

"They're veterans," sad Ernie Ayana, who served in the Army in Vietnam with a dog named Heidi at his side. "No doubt about that."

Ayana, who is the Army sentry director for the Vietnam Dog Handlers Association, joined other military personnel, police and history buffs for the dedication of the fort's newly refurbished canine cemetery.

American flags marked the spots on freshly laid grass where many of the dogs are buried, their names etched in metal plaques. There's Cheetah, Lothar and Fritz. Exactly how many are there nobody knows because early records cannot be found.

Paul Acosta knew many of those dogs. He worked with them when he was guarding a Nike missile site in northern Los Angeles County. His own companion, Brutus, is also buried there, but his marker was stolen long ago, leaving no trace as to his exact location.

Acosta was teamed up with the German shepherd during military police training. They quickly formed a strong bond.

"He was smarter than I was," Acosta said. "They'd tell us to turn left, but I'd turn right. But Brutus turned left. I spent more time with him than my wife."

The ceremony featured salutes, a moment of silence and taps.

For those who came to pay their respects, the animals deserved all the pomp they received.

That it happened at Fort MacArthur was appropriate: The facility is where the first military dogs were trained nearly 70 years ago.

"This is a fitting tribute," Acosta said. "These dogs deserve it. They contributed to people who wanted to serve their country."

Ayana estimated that 100,000 men and women owe their lives to the dogs, which were used as sentries, bomb sniffers, booby-trap finders and scouts.

"If a scout dog didn't catch a trip wire, the dog and the handler both blew up. They saved GIs that were left in battle. Those dogs found them."

The small plot had been largely neglected until a group of volunteers decided a few years ago that it needed to be fixed up. With the guidance of Dorothy Matich, they raised about $40,000 for the effort.

"They're veterans," she said of the dogs. "Nobody asked them. They were brought in and trained. They deserve a little spot."

If the dogs are remembered warmly now, they were mostly considered unnecessary by the military after they were no longer needed – and most of them were euthanized. Of the 4,000 sent to Vietnam, only a few hundred were shipped home.

"It wasn't appropriate," said Steve Nelson, curator of the Fort MacArthur Museum.

But the Army has since changed its policy and the animals are now retrained and given new homes at the end of their military careers.

"They fought for our freedom," said San Pedro resident Flo Kleinjan. "They fought with our soldiers. People don't realize the service they performed."

D-Day

(First published in 2004)

Men like Robert Brigham and Bill Woodcock didn't know they were part of something historic – they were too busy trying to stay alive.

The two men were among the 150,000 soldiers who participated in the D-Day invasion of France that began on June 6, 1944. One arrived by air and the other by sea, but both came within inches of dying in the fierce battles between Allied and German troops on the beaches of northern France.

Before the smoke cleared that day, some 10,000 people died or were wounded.

To commemorate the 60th anniversary of one of World

War II's most important – and bloodiest – battles, Brigham joined other area veterans for a ceremony on the SS Lane Victory in San Pedro, Calif.

Brigham, a North Dakota native, set sail from southern England on June 5. To where, the young Army private didn't know.

"At 6 a.m., they were boarding us on trucks in Southampton" he said. "Then they loaded us on ships. We had no idea where we were going."

Even as he approached the beaches of Normandy, Brigham still wasn't told what to expect. But he and the other men on the transport bided their time as best they could.

"We sat around and played cards," the 81-year-old said. "They had us stacked like sardines. There wasn't nothing else we could do."

Brigham was lucky enough to miss the first wave of the invasion, where men were picked off easily. By the time he arrived on June 7 – D-Day Plus One – the fighting had moved off the beach, but the front was still within the range of a tank. Allied forces had taken over most of the beach the previous night.

"We could hear it," he said. "There was no mistaking what was going on."

Many men drowned before they ever reached the shore. Riding a Higgins Boat, a wide transport with an end that swung open, Brigham had to wade across several hundred feet of treacherous water before he reached land. As soon as he jumped off the transport, he found himself standing in water up to his chest.

"It was awfully scary," he said. "I was scared of water to begin with. I couldn't swim. My weapon got wet. What the hell do you do when water almost comes over your head."

His troubles were only beginning. Once on land, a man standing nearby stepped on a land mind. Brigham saw his leg explode. It's an image that will always stay with him.

"There was nothing you can do to help the guy," he said. "I don't know how to explain it."

Brigham was later captured by the Germans near Paris and spent months in prisoner of war camps and digging ditches for German shelters until he was rescued in April 1945. After his discharge later that year, Brigham said he started drinking.

"I tried to drown my troubles, but they wouldn't drown," he said.

After the war, he met his wife, Pat, who died two years ago. They had one son who lives out of state. Brigham worked at a Northrop machine shop until he retired in 1982.

Nearly 3 million military personnel were needed to pull it off the invasion. Supporting them were 5,000 ships, 4,000 landing craft and more than 11,000 aircraft.

The beach landing was preceded by a night drop behind the German coastal defenses. Among those hitting the beach by air was Bill Woodcock. The British Columbia native, now 87, flew a glider filled with troops as part of the British Royal Air Force.

"I looked out of the plane and didn't see any action," he recalled. "What war? There was no war going on. But as we turned around we got hit by flak and we had to bail out."

Woodcock landed in the water and swam ashore. Others on his plane weren't so lucky.

"I just scraped my nose and got a little scratch mark," he said. "The wireless operator with me, he drowned. I guess he couldn't swim. He hollered, but he was gone by the time I got there to save him."

Woodcock found refuge with some locals who lived nearby.

"I was right in the front," he said. "I joined up with these French people and stayed all night in a barn. I was soaking wet."

The next day, he headed back out to the front with a group of British commandos who found him in the barn.

"All kinds of crap was going on," he said. "The battleships in the water were firing these big rockets inland. I sat in a landing craft watching them. I wanted to get back to England. I thought, 'Boy, I got this far. I want to get back to England.' "

For Bob Johnson, who helped organize the tribute , honoring D- Day veterans is a good way to thank them for all they've done. Johnson, a Vietnam-era veteran, happened to have been born on June 6, 1945, a year to the day after the invasion.

"After 60 years, we want to give a very special tribute to those in the South Bay to honor the sacrifices they made to help preserve freedom in the world and rid Europe of Nazi tyranny," he said. "I'm pleased I could do a small part to bring them together for what could be a last hurrah for a lot of them."

For members of the French Consulate in Los Angeles, celebrating the dwindling number of men who helped liberate their country only makes sense.

"It was the end of the darkest period in our history," said Deputy Gen. Consul Olivier Plancon. "The gratitude to the Allied troops and Americans is still extremely high in France. Every year it's a celebration for us. Monuments to D-Day are everywhere."

Plancon said that even though relations between the United States and France have been strained recently, the feelings of affection continue to run deep.

"What the United States did cannot be forgotten," he said. "That's what we want to highlight. We share a friendship that has been alive for more than 200 years. That is what really matters."

While they knew they were doing something important, it wasn't until they got home that many of the men who fought in D-Day realized that they were participating in an event that would alter the course of history.

"I didn't realize it at the time," Brigham said. "It doesn't even enter your mind. Afterwards I realized it. When I got back here and started thinking about it, then I knew it was big – really, really big."

In Search of Their Fathers

(First published in 2003)

Eleven years ago, Tony Cordero came to a sad realization: He was to about turn 30, reaching an age his father never attained.

He'd no longer be able to use his dad as a guidepost.

His father, Maj. William Cordero, an Air Force navigator, died in 1965 on a mission in Vietnam. Tony Cordero was 4 years old.

"Everyone has singled out that day they outlive their dad," the 41-year-old said. "We grow up with the experience. The void is always there. I wondered if other people felt the same way."

Other people did feel the same way. Lots of people.

Now, about 80 of them are set to embark on a journey back to Vietnam, a place where world events shaped their lives, where their fathers went and never returned.

"The reason for us going is to see where our dads served, to see the people and the country they fought and died for," Cordero said.

In 1990, Cordero started looking around for others in his situation, people who lost a parent in the war. This was before the Internet, so his search meant hours on the telephone with veterans groups and weeks waiting for letters to be returned.

"I wondered if other people felt the same way," he said. "I called around to see if there were other organizations, but there weren't."

So Cordero started Sons and Daughters in Touch, a nonprofit organization that helps children of people lost in Vietnam stay in contact.

"Because there was no other organization like this, we built it as we went along," he said. "Like it or not, I've been thrust into the role of leader of this whole movement."

The trip is not about finding peace; Cordero has that. He's married with four children. His mother remarried and he has a strong relationship with her husband. Instead, the trip, set to begin March 5, is about history and honor.

"There's enough closure, I already have that," Cordero

said. "But while you can never get over it, you can come to terms with it and understand how it shaped you."

But there are moments when a look flashes across Cordero's face, moments when he thinks about watching his own children grow up or when he thinks about things his own father missed.

"It's not hard talking about unless I think about what I missed here," he said tapping a faded black notebook with worn edges.

Inside are pictures of his father, a man who looks like he could be Cordero's younger brother. There are service patches, bawdy song lyrics that his father and his buddies must have sung together, pictures of his family – the kinds of things that most people take for granted.

"The biggest thing we do is honor our fathers and others who served," he said. "We're not like the (Veterans Administration) where you get counseling. We're a resource. We're here to help locate military records or help obtain information about scholarships."

A few people joined the group in the early years, but after a story appeared in Parade magazine, membership jumped to 3,500. At the annual event in 2000, they decided it was time to take a Vietnam trip.

"The war is over," he said. "It's time for us to recognize Vietnam as a country, not an event. It became evident that the time was ripe to explore a trip."

It took two years to get everything in order and arrangements made. Among the largest supporters of the trips are other Vietnam veterans, who feel proud that the group is taking such a step all these decades later.

Jan Scruggs, the man who came up with the idea for the Vietnam Veterans Memorial in Washington, D.C., said the participants would come back changed people.

"It will rekindle in each of them a desire for some real historical perspective to the entire Vietnam experience," he said. "It's going to show them the meaning of what this sacrifice was."

Not many others have ventured across the ocean like the Sons and Daughters have, said Scruggs, whose group, the Vietnam Veterans Memorial Fund, will be conducting a memorial service in Vietnam for the visitors.

"There's never been this large a group of people affected in such a profound way that's returned to Vietnam," he said. "I have a very good feeling about it. Things like this really help the process of healing. I'm predicting that the Sons and Daughters will find that Vietnam is a very lovely and very peaceful place as well. It's a place where many veterans return and put many of their ghosts to rest."

Cordero has few memories of his father. He remembers running through sugar cane fields with him when the family lived in the Philippines, but not much else.

"The worst thing that happens in war is little kids lose their dads," he said.

But although his father wasn't there to guide him through life, he still left something of a legacy.

"I know what my dad left behind," he said. "I know

what he didn't experience. I know what he missed. My dad didn't teach me how to drive, but I got to teach my kids. It made me a better father."

Once in Vietnam, the visitors will break into small groups and venture into the jungles to the exact spots where their dads died.

"If I saw wheels and a tail section and I knew this is where my life changed forever, I don't know how I'd handle that," he said. "This should be their glory years. They should be leading families and the country. But our fathers didn't have that chance."

Finally At Rest

(First published in 2006)

As soon as she heard the telephone pierce the quiet of the night, Carolee Chubb could tell an unwelcome message was on its way. There was something about the way it sounded, something that augured a change for everybody in her family.

"It was an uncanny feeling," she said. "The phone sounded angry. I don't know how to explain it. It had to be bad news."

The call was from her husband's parents. Their youngest child had been shot down over the jungles of Laos. John Chubb was dead. Although only 20, his life was over. But for his family, an ordeal was just beginning, one they would have to endure for nearly 35 years.

It took that long, but in 2006, as surviving family members, aging longtime friends and fellow Vietnam War-era veterans gathered at cemetery, Army Pfc. John Jacobsen Chubb was finally laid to rest.

Given the honors of a military funeral, John's remains, which have long been lost in a southeast Asian jungle, were placed in a vault where his parents are interred. His family could finally say goodbye.

"I have always been proud of you," his brother Cliff Chubb wrote for the occasion. "Let go of your fear and anger. I will try, too."

* * *

Ron Erwin held up a black-and-white picture. A group of kids are standing on the street. The boys have their hair shorn close to the heads in crew cuts. The girls are in party dresses.

"That's John's sixth birthday party," he said pointing at the smiling faces. "That's me. That's John. We were in Cub Scouts together. We got into trouble together."

Now 55, with a thick mane of gray hair, Erwin remembers the last time he saw his buddy riding a motorcycle.

"He was really at peace with himself," Erwin said. "He was going to do his duty."

John Chubb was born on Dec. 9, 1950.

He was dyslexic, but good with his hands and had a passion for fixing and restoring cars. There was the 1948 Pontiac, the 1949 Cadillac and the 1957 Chevrolet Nomad.

At the funeral, friends laughed that before he could drive, he had a custom-painted Schwinn Stingray bicycle.

"He was into karate and weightlifting. He was good looking and had an easy way about him," Cliff said.

"He had a lot of girlfriends," he said. "He was a happy-go-lucky kid."

He would stand by his friends if there was trouble, but he preferred to charm his way out of a fight. The only time he ever lost his temper was when he was having trouble fixing a car.

"Nobody got hurt when he was around," Cliff said. "Not even the bad guys. He'd go away feeling bad, but not hurt."

Losing his younger brother wasn't easy for Cliff. There was lingering guilt and bouts of depression. It's hard for him to talk about it.

"He always tried to protect his brother," said his wife, Carolee. "He felt like he failed him. He was the big brother and he was supposed to protect his little brother."

But Cliff takes comfort in knowing that his brother died protecting others.

"They saved a lot of people," he said. "And those people saved a bunch of people. How do you figure that?"

* * *

It was the height of the Vietnam War. People his age were doing anything to stay out of harm's way, but John wanted to enlist.

"He was very patriotic," said Gloria Lyons, who met John in the seventh grade and dated him for years. She said the two became engaged before he shipped overseas in 1970.

"One thing that stands out in my mind is we were in the 11th grade and a teacher dropped a flag on the floor. John argued with him because he wouldn't burn it. He got suspended."

Jim McMahon came from Kentucky to attend the service. He and John met in high school and were inseparable until McMahon joined the Air Force. Now a professional pilot, he remembered the last time the two ever spoke was when John dropped him off for his tour of duty.

"We sat in his Nomad and drank hot chocolate," he said. "I said, 'see you when it's over.' Those were the last words. I've not gone many days when I haven't thought about John."

But it wasn't until years later that things really began to sink in.

"I was at a Christmas party in 1986," McMahon said. "I had a wonderful job, a beautiful wife. Life just came together for me. And something just hit me and I went to the hall and I cried like a baby. I'm here and he's not. He's missing this."

Last Letter Home

* * *

After training, John was sent to Vietnam, where he was a gunner on a Huey helicopter. On March 20, 1971 – just three weeks after he arrived in the war zone – the helicopter was shot down while on a rescue mission in the Savannakhet Province of Laos. Three other men died with him – all from the Army 101st Airborne Division. They were Maj. Jack L. Barker, Capt. John F. Dugan and Sgt. William Dillender. Those three, along with remains that couldn't be identified, will be buried at Arlington National Cemetery.

The ill-fated mission and the efforts to return the remains are recounted in the book, "Where They Lay," by Earl Swift. This is how he described the last minutes of the crew's lives.

"The flak started miles out. The Huey's pilots slalomed the bird among arcing yellow tracers and blooms of brown smoke as it dropped toward the target. Its gunners opened fire with their M-60s, sweeping the trees on the helicopter's final approach.

"The reply was overwhelming: Bullets raked the chopper's thin metal skin, whistled into the cabin and tore into man and machine. Then came something worse – a blur, rising from the trees, a telltale plume – and a flash. Fire swallowed the Huey. It hit the ground in pieces."

John was awarded the Silver Star and Bronze Star, along with a Purple Heart for his efforts that day.

* * *

There are still 1,807 Americans unaccounted for from the Vietnam War. Of those, 364 were lost in Laos.

From 1988 to 2000, joint teams from the United States and the Lao People's Democratic Republic searched several times for the remains. Surveys in recent years found the Huey's wreckage and some remains, which were identified late last year by forensic anthropologists using medical and dental records.

Seeking out remains of fallen soldiers has not always been a top priority for the government, said Larry Greer, a spokesman for the Pentagon's POW-MIA Office. Efforts began after World War II and gained momentum after the Vietnam War, he said.

"The payoff is to this serviceman and (the) family," Greer said. "It recognizes the pain they still endure. It doesn't make the pain go away, but at least they know the story, they know what happened. So many of the older family members went to their graves not knowing."

John's father died in 1980 and his mother in 1981. Not being able to put him to rest haunted them until the end.

"There was always a sadness that never went away," Cliff said. "Their wish was that John would have a place. They bought a niche for him. Dad passed and no John. Mom died a year later and still no John. Why did they have to wait so long?"

The pain of losing his brother will never go away. But

Cliff Chubb said that the family can now begin to find some peace.

"John will cuddle next to Dad and things will be better," he said.

Worth a Thousand Words

(First published in 2006)

Where it's been the past 143 years, nobody knows. But a rare Civil War picture that proves camels once served in the U.S. Army is finally heading home to the place it was first photographed: the Drum Barracks Civil War Museum in Wilmington. Calif.

The grainy, splotched, black-and-white image measures a scant 4 1/4-by-2 1/2 inches. But when museum director Susan Ogle heard it was being sold on an Internet auction site, she knew she had to have it.

"I found out about it the minute it went on eBay," Ogle said. "I got six phone calls the first day. 'Have you seen? Have you seen?' "

The picture didn't come cheap. Competition was stiff and late bidding pushed the selling price to $4,569.63. But Ogle said it was worth it.

The image itself is well known. A copy already resides in the Drum Barracks, and versions of it also exist at University of Southern California, the Los Angeles Public Library and the Huntington Library. But the one Ogle bought may be the one all the others were copied from, making it both historically and aesthetically important.

"If you've ever looked at these old pictures, they have a unique quality to them," Ogle said. "There is a depth and richness to the print. It's like looking at a print of the Mona Lisa and then at the original. It's two different things."

Ogle, who has a master's degree in art history with a concentration in photography, won't know for sure until she examines the photo. But she said the seller is reputable and she has three days to return the photograph if it turns out to be a copy.

"I won't know until I get my hands on it," she said. "But from what I've seen (all the others) look retouched. The eBay one doesn't look retouched. We have to compare the images and try to see what came from where. All these little strings will pull together."

Using camels as transport vehicles was proposed in the 1850s by Secretary of War Jefferson Davis, who would later switch sides to become president of the Confederacy. Although camels can carry far more than a mule, they can also be unruly, so the experiment was abandoned, but not before two shiploads of them arrived from Turkey and Egypt.

After moving around a bit, three dozen wound up at the Drum Barracks in early 1862. They left a little more than a year later and were auctioned off to private parties.

The back of the photo incorrectly identifies the location as "quartermaster department, San Pedro." And it was once in a collection owned by photographer C.C. Pierce, who claimed to have taken it, but he didn't arrive in Southern California until years after the camels left.

"He would copy negatives and would publish them," said Jennifer Watts, curator of photographs at the Huntington Library.

Ogle believes the image was probably not taken by a professional.

"I'm thinking it's a good possibility it was taken by a military photographer, but we don't have any information anywhere that nails the photographer down."

As far as spending thousands of dollars for the image, Watts said it was money well spent.

"Given what it is and in terms of the unusual subject matter and the early date of the image, that's quite reasonable," she said. "You get to see if someone made alterations to the negative at the time or if things have been cropped out over the years."

Los Angeles historian Brady Westwater did his own research on the image. He said that even though he has books with the picture in it, he'd love to have the original.

"If it's the only Civil War camel photo around, you want to own that," he said. "If I had the money, I would have bought it."

Ogle's bid, which was made by a computer-savvy friend, came in the auction's last few seconds. Before that, 30 others were placed.

"You've got the Civil War people, who are rabid," Watts said. "And you've got people interested in early Los Angeles. They're also a feverish bunch."

Ogle won't say how much she was willing to pay if the price continued to soar.

"I'm not going to tell you," she said. "I've had an awful lot of people ask me that."

Spending the money for the photo wasn't in the museum's budget, but Ogle is confident of recouping the expense.

"We're raising funds," she said. "We've already gotten donations."

Names

(First published in 2006)

Of the 58,249 men and women who died during the Vietnam War, 19 were born on Sept. 17, 1949.

Bob Gilles didn't know a single one of them, but he was born that day, too. And so on his second trip to the Vietnam Veterans Memorial, Gilles rubbed all their names onto the white stripes of an American flag. The names are faded now, but he raises it outside his home every year on his birthday to honor them.

"I had my 19th birthday in Vietnam," he said. "There happened to be 19 guys on the wall with my same birthday."

Looking at the flag now is an emotional experience for

Gilles. More than 30 years after he returned as an Army soldier, it's something that's still difficult for him to talk about.

"I don't know all their names, and that's hard to deal with," he said. "I had to recognize those guys somehow because they aren't here any longer. I don't think any of them wanted to die."

Gilles has also collected rubbings of the men whose names he remembers – 54 of them – friends whose memory he protects fiercely.

"There's Howie, John. ... Howie was the first friend that I ever had to put on a chopper in a body bag," he said, his voice cracking. "You don't get over it. You don't forget."

But Gilles was haunted by the memories of the men whose names have faded from his memory. So, in 1990, he traveled to the memorial in Washington, D.C., and made the rubbings.

"For me, it's the names of the men I don't know," he said. "And I don't know how to find them."

These are private matters for Gilles and he doesn't like to discuss them. He believes Memorial Day should be about the fallen, not the men like him who came home to restart their lives. Calling attention to himself is something he's uncomfortable with.

"Memorial Day is to honor the guys who have sacrificed all for the freedoms we have," he said. "And we have so many freedoms."

Gilles credits his wife, Carol, and son, Matthew, who is

studying to become a commercial pilot, with helping get him through some rough spots.

"They've been with me a long time," he said.

Gilles is 56, an age when connecting with his past is important. It wasn't that way when he returned from Vietnam.

"The fact is you didn't want to remember names," he said. "I never celebrated my birthday, but at least I learned to appreciate it a little more."

Remembering the names of men he served with was made more difficult by a habit among soldiers to call each other by nicknames.

"That way, if you lost them, it was a way of not getting close," he said. "And now, some of them you only remember that way."

Gilles said serving in a war connects people in ways that are hard for others to understand.

"Civilians will never get a flavor of it," he said. "If I can help somebody else in discovering how to remember, that is the thing I want to get across."

Almost every soldier knew people he can vaguely remember. Even if they were never acquainted.

"These are guys I didn't know, but they did serve," he said. "Somehow doing this is about remembering them. Memorial Day is remembering those guys I knew, even if I never met them."

One More Mile

(First published in 2007)

After coming back from Iraq late last year, Ed Acevedo wanted to do something to show his support for the military men and women who served there.

A civilian construction project manager who was doing work in the Middle East, Acevedo knew only that he didn't want to have anything to do with the division and discord that he encountered when he returned to the States.

"I saw bickering and political wrangling," said the 41-year-old Army veteran. "It was Democrats vs. Republicans. I wanted to do something nonpolitical. This is such a polarizing era."

And then an idea came to him:

"One day I bought a big, blue bicycle and decided to ride to California," he said.

And just like that, with virtually no long-distance riding under his belt, he left his home in St. Augustine, Fla., and headed west to raise awareness for those who have suffered disabilities in the war.

"Before I go back to the Middle East, I'd like to do something to help," Acevedo said. "I like the symbolism of 'the long road' and 'one more mile.' It's symbolic for the long road injured vets have to travel."

Acevedo has no sponsorship. The cost is coming out of his own pocket and the charity of friends and strangers.

And he personally collects no money along the way. He stops at veterans hospitals, American Legion halls and newspaper offices and asks people to give money to established charities.

"I've connected with a lot of young military people and older veterans," he said. "I've helped collect about $15,000 to $20,000. That's more than when I started."

Traveling 60 to 80 miles a day, Acevedo said he's lost about 10 pounds on his 4,400-mile trek. He sleeps in campgrounds or at friends' houses. And he eats anywhere – and anything – he can.

"I eat as much as possible," he said. "I'll walk into a store and walk out with Rice Krispies Treats and raspberry Twizzlers. There's no harm. I'll burn it off."

The worst thing that's happened to him on the trip was falling into a ditch. The best thing might have been when he went on a bike ride with disabled veterans at Camp Pendleton. He was going to stop his journey in San Diego, but after that, he decided to keep going all the way north to Vancouver, British Columbia. And he is thinking about riding all the way back to Florida.

"If I don't run out of warm weather, I'll consider it," he said. "I want to do one thing that doesn't have an agenda. I've seen the real America."

Bells

(First published in 2004)

Roy Abbot.

Clang.

Albert Adams.

Clang.

Lloyd Reeves read the names in alphabetical order. Between each, he paused briefly and pulled on a rope that rang a small bell. Standing on top of a miniature submarine he built himself, he read 81 names of nearly forgotten sailors who died exactly 60 years earlier.

The sun danced on the water and tiny waves splashed on the side of his craft. Aside from a pack of seals barking on a nearby barge, the harbor was eerily quiet as the minutes passed.

Frank Corey.

Clang.

Elmer Crain Jr.

Clang.

Reeves was honoring men who died 10 years before he was born. The USS Trout left Midway Island on Feb. 19, 1944 on its way to patrol the China Coast. It was never heard from again and was presumed lost on April 17. It was later learned that the Trout was involved in a battle with a Japanese ship and was lost on Leap Day.

"They had way more moxie," Reeves said. "They just started firing away."

Reeves normally uses his boat – a replica of another lost World War II submarine – to take people on tours of the dock. The third-scale submarine can seat three inside and another three on top. During cruises, they swap places for the chance to sit at a set of circular windows in the bottom of the boat that allows them to see what's going on under the water: swirling plants and bright orange garibaldi darting through the breakwater.

They can also see a few artifacts posted to the wall, including an aging telegram informing a family that their loved one was presumed dead. But because the activities of submarines were closely guarded secrets, the letter made no mention of how or where the sailor met his fate.

The telegram turned out to be premature, because the man turned up after the war in a Japanese concentration camp.

Reeves comes to the marina every weekend from his home in Morro Bay.

But on this day, Reeves was alone. He put the word out to local veterans that he would be performing a tolling of the bells, but by departing time, none arrived.

"Every year there are less and less of them," Reeves said.

Albert Lewis.

Clang.

Joseph Magner.

Clang.

Duty on a submarine was dangerous and many were lost during the war. Reeves goes out about once a month to honor the crew of a different sub.

"I don't know why I do it," he said. "These guys aren't around and I'd like to remember them."

He used to have a hard time getting through a list without breaking up, but now he focuses on the sound of the bell.

The ceremony took just a few minutes. When he was done, he turned around and headed back to dock.

William Winter.

Clang.

H.E. Woodworth.

Clang.

About the Author

Josh Grossberg has been a journalist for nearly 30 years. His work has been published in such far-flung places as the Los Angeles Times to the Kurdistan Times. His articles have received local, state, and national recognition, including the Associated Press, California Newspaper Publishers Association, the Copley Ring of Truth and the Los Angeles Press Club.

Josh is the author of From "Scamp to Champ: How One Puppy Gave Hope to the Blind and other Animal Stories."

He currently works as an editor and reporter at a daily newspaper near his home in Los Angeles.

If you have a story to tell, email Josh at info@lastletterhome.org

About Tom Lasser

Lt. Col. Thomas Edward Lasser retired after completing 40 years of military service. He spent seven years on active duty with the US Army and another 33 years with the California National Guard. Thirty years of that which was full-time status with the California Military Department. Tom is a Vietnam veteran. He is now consulting for his own firm, T. E. Lasser & Associates, LLC.

He earned his Army aviator wings after completing the Army Aviation Warrant Officer Aviator Flight Course. He flew UH-1 Hueys in the Republic of Vietnam and after receiving a direct commission, he completed another tour in Vietnam flying Boeing CH-47 Chinooks. Tom then transferred into the California Army National Guard following his second tour of combat duty.

Tom has commanded at the company and battalion levels also serving in a variety of staff positions including Headquarters, California National Guard in Sacramento.

He is a master Army aviator with over 6000 flying hours including more than 1000 helicopter missions in Vietnam and almost 1800 combat flying hours.

His military decorations include the Distinguished Flying Cross ,Purple Heart, Legion of Merit, Air Medal with 35 Oak Leaf clusters, Meritorious Service Medals, Bronze Star and other commendations, service awards and campaign ribbons which reflect over forty years of military service. Unit awards include the Valorous Unit Award, Army Superior Unit Award and Vietnamese Cross of Gallantry.

Tom is a life member of the Military Order of the Purple Heart, VFW, American Legion and the Military Officers Association of America.